# Excellence
# in
# Upper-Level Writing

# 2017/2018

**The Gayle Morris**
**Sweetland Center for Writing**

Edited by
Dana Nichols

Published in 2018 by Michigan Publishing
University of Michigan Library

Michigan Publishing
1210 Buhr Building
839 Greene Street
Ann Arbor, MI 48104
lib.pod@umich.edu


ISBN 978-1-60785-491-3

# Table of Contents
*Excellence in Upper-Level Writing*

# Excellence in Upper-Level Writing 2017/2018

**Sweetland Writing Prize Chair**

Dana Nichols

**Sweetland Writing Prize Committee**

Angie Berkley

Jimmy Brancho

Cat Cassel

Raymond McDaniel

Dana Nichols

Carol Tell

**Sweetland Writing Prize Judges**

Sahin Acikgoz

Jimmy Brancho

Sigrid Cordell

Michael Makin

Bruce Mannheim

Jillian Myers

Kyra Pazan

Adriana Ponce

Rachna Reddy

Colleen Seifert

Matthew Solomon

Rachel Webb

Jana Wilbricht

Sunhay You

**Administrative Support**

Laura Schulyer

Aaron Valdez

# Winners List

**Granader Family Prize for Excellence in Upper-Level Writing (Sciences)**

Evan Hoopingarner "Unreliable inhaler access plagues Detroit's asthmatics"
*Nominated by Emilia Askari, Environ 320: Environmental Journalism: Reporting
about Science, Policy and Public Health*

Deirdre McGovern "What We Learn from the Mouse"
*Nominated by Andrew Bernard, Anthrbio 368: Primate Social Behavior*


**Granader Family Prize for Excellence in Upper-Level Writing (Social Sciences)**

Jessica Baer "Modern Sports as Pre-Modern in Media"
*Nominated by Emma Waitzman (GSI) & Andrei Markovits (Faculty),
PolSci 368: Sports, Politics, and Society*

Kyra Lyngklip "Polarization and Lobbying Influence of the Dodd-Frank Act"
*Nominated by Eitan Paul (GSI) & Nancy Burns (Faculty),
PolSci 381: Political Research Design*


**Granader Family Prize for Excellence in Upper-Level Writing (Humanities)**

Mateusz Borowiecki "Human Agency and Control in the
Shadow of Enlightenment"
*Nominated by Scott Spector, German 401: European Intellectual and Cultural
History from Revolution to World War*

Caitlyn Zawideh "Mother of Exiles"
*Nominated by Molly Beer, English 325: The Art of the Essay*

# Nominees List

| Student Name | Instructor Name |
| --- | --- |
| Livvy Arau-McSweeney | Jennifer Metsker |
| Shaylyn Austin | Julie Halpert |
| Jessica Baer | Emma Waitzman |
| Adela Baker | Christine Modey |
| Ashley Bock | Jennifer Metsker |
| Nathanael Boorsma | Kevin Miller |
| Mateusz Borowiecki | Scott Spector |
| Brooke Callahan | Julie Halpert |
| Katharine Carroll | Emily Saidel |
| Ryan Chin | Allison Alexy |
| Joseph Costello | Molly Beer |
| Mark Dovich | Eitan Paul |
| Meghan Harrington | Ben Finkel |
| Evan Hoopingarner | Emilia Askari |
| Anna Horton | Christine Modey |
| Aaron Howell | Jared Eno |
| Chetali Jain | Gary Huffnagle |
| Nakora Kowal | Allison Alexy |
| Kyra Lyngklip | Eitan Paul |
| Jeremy Lynn | T Hetzel |
| Deirdre McGovern | Andrew Bernard |
| Margaret O'Connor | John Rubadeau |
| Alena Olsen | Emilia Askari |
| Kristina Perkins | T Hetzel |
| Henry Poggi | John Rubadeau |
| Christine Rysenga | Andrew Bernard |
| Emma Urbain | Kevin Miller |
| Caitlyn Zawideh | Molly Beer |

# Introduction

One of the two writing courses required of all graduates in the College of Literature, Science, and the Arts is an Upper-Level Writing course. These courses, offered by approximately 36 different departments and programs across the College, provide an introduction to the ways of writing in a given field. Many students complete upper-level courses in their majors, but a good number choose to fulfill the requirement in another department because they want to broaden their experiences as writers. Wherever they take it, students have many opportunities to hone their writerly craft in the upper-level course.

Instructors in upper-level writing courses give students opportunities to write regularly, receive helpful feedback, and develop ever more effective ways of making strong evidence-based arguments. The assignments included with each selection show another way that instructors contribute to the development of their student writers. By carefully designing assignments that make expectations clear, calling for meaning-making, requiring revisions, and encouraging students to reflect on their own ideas and ways of writing, instructors help students grow as writers.

But the best instruction in the world doesn't matter unless students take it up. The students included here took best advantage of what their instructors offered. They wrote drafts and then addressed suggestions from peers and instructors as they revised and edited their writing until it satisfied them. As they revised, they considered their audiences, looked for ways to clarify their central ideas, and devised ways to make their prose both clear and compelling. As the selections included here show, upper-division students, with the support of their instructors and a challenging curriculum, succeeded in producing very effective prose.

Nearly every day we hear calls, from business, from government, and from everyday people, for better writers. "They just can't write," is a common lament.

The students whose work is represented here provide a response to that lament because they are well prepared to write for a wide variety of audiences and purposes.

A generous gift from the Granader family provides a cash award for each student writer. This, along with a certificate recognizing their excellence in writing, gives prize-winning students tangible evidence of the importance of writing well. At the same time, these students provide a model and inspiration for their peers. *Excellence in Upper-Level Writing 2018* will join volumes from past years in an online format where it can be used by ULWR instructors and in other courses.

Many thanks are due to Dana Nichols for her careful editing of this volume and to Aaron Valdez for creating a design worthy of excellent writing. Selecting the winning essays from among the many nominations was not an easy task, but it was taken up by participants in the Sweetland Seminar, a group of faculty and graduate students committed to integrating writing into their courses and helping students become better writers. The judges for the Granader Family Prize for Excellence in Upper-Level Writing were Sahin Acikgoz, Jimmy Brancho, Sigrid Cordell, Michael Makin, Bruce Mannheim, Jillian Myers, Kyra Pazan, Adriana Ponce, Rachna Reddy, Colleen Seifert, Matthew Solomon, Rachel Webb, Jana Wilbricht, and Sunhay You.

I am grateful to all of these judges for making the difficult choices involved in selecting the winners of this year's prizes.

Anne Ruggles Gere, Director
Sweetland Center for Writing

# Winning Essays
## Granader Prize for Excellence in Upper-Level Writing (sciences)

## Unreliable inhaler access plagues Detroit's asthmatics

by Evan Hoopingarner

*From Environ 320: Environmental Journalism: Reporting about Science, Policy and Public Health*

Nominated by Emilia Askari

Evan Hoopingarner's news feature about the black market for asthma inhalers in a low-income Detroit neighborhood is well-reported and elegantly written. The story explores the life-threatening choices made by people who can't afford adequate asthma medication while living in the 48217 zip code, which has one of the highest levels of air pollution in the country. As Evan reveals, these people sometimes buy used asthma inhalers, figuring they are better than nothing. It's a problem that is easily ignored, without people such as Evan who force readers to take a hard look. "Physicians often aren't aware of major barriers to care such as cost, transportation to pharmacies, and ineffective information transfer to patients," Evan writes. He is interested in a career in science. Evan displayed empathy, courage and strong news instincts as he reported this story in the shadow of the Marathon oil refinery. His first-hand account of the sights and people of this impoverished neighborhood is written with a direct style that draws attention to this major public health problem. Evan's piece deftly combines the account of an asthma sufferer, the perspective of a city worker trying to address poor access to asthma inhalers, and statistics to tell a persuasive story. I am very pleased to nominate Evan Hoopingarner and his news feature, "Unreliable inhaler access plagues Detroit's asthmatics," for a 2017 Sweetland prize.

*Emilia Askari*

# Unreliable inhaler access plagues Detroit's asthmatics

The surgical mask is a relatively new part of Emma Lockridge's bedtime routine. With tar sands oil being processed a few blocks away from her home, the mask prevents particulate matter from getting into her lungs and irritating her asthma. Winters are even harder for the longtime asthmatic. "With all this fog, the air cannot rise, and stays on top of us and our homes and our lives," she says. "I'm suffering right now due to the impact of Marathon Petroleum."

Lockridge isn't alone. In Detroit, a combination of poverty and pollution has created a population of poor asthmatics who are driven to unconventional means of obtaining medicine. Whether it's relying on the leftover medicines of friends and family, constant emergency room visits, or even turning to a small black market, Detroit's residents are often forced to go to great lengths in order to breathe.

Neighborhoods in southwest Detroit are interspersed with heavy industries, such as Marathon Petroleum's Detroit Refinery, coal plants, and steel mills, which pump out an incredible amount of pollution next to homes and schools. This area is home to the state's most polluted zip code, as well as some of the only areas in Michigan that are in non-attainment for sulfur dioxide, meaning the levels of this pollutant make the air unhealthy to breathe. Here, 1 in 6 people have asthma. But with 2 in 5 living in poverty, access to proper care is extremely difficult.

When asthmatics seek medical attention, they often find that their symptoms are treated, but the root causes of those symptoms are ignored. "We have some great doctors and great physicians out there, but we're not catching everything," says Elizabeth Milton, an asthma educator in the Detroit area. As part of her work, she regularly counsels children and adults who are on Medicaid to help them understand and manage their asthma.

Milton recalls a seven-year-old patient who lived two blocks from the Marathon refinery. "The doctors were increasing his inhaler constantly, but never thought to ask: What's going on? Where does he live? That's critical information, that you are exposed on a daily basis to sulfur dioxide."

Representatives from Marathon Petroleum could not be reached for comment.

According to Milton, improved treatment of asthmatics will require a shift in mindset as well as a willingness to ask critical questions. "People respond to asthma as if it's an acute situation, and not a chronic situation," says Milton. "Emergency room doctors are there to treat acute situations. But if you're treating that same person for the same problem 6 times, it's time to make a change in how you treat that patient."

Physicians often aren't aware of major barriers to care such as cost, transportation to pharmacies, and ineffective information transfer to patients. "These are very small questions," says Milton. "It wouldn't take much time, but it might make a difference."

Although progress is being made in both patient and physician education, there are still needs that the current medical system doesn't fulfill. For many, compared to conventional means, sharing medication is cheaper, easier, and may be their only option. "There has been more than one occasion where I've called somebody up who I know has an inhaler," says Rhonda Anderson, a lifelong Detroit resident and organizer for the Sierra Club.

According to Lockridge, various environmental factors can cause periods of reduced symptoms, which might result in "a few extra puffs" left in an inhaler or nebulizer before the prescription's renewal or expiration date. On the other hand, says Milton, during periods of frequent flare-ups, "that inhaler will not last through the month." During times between refills, Milton says that her clients "do access other venues to get medication. That's where you see sharing."

In addition to sharing medication, some have to resort to further measures. "When you're talking about such a desperate condition, not being able to breathe, it can literally drive a person to do all sorts of things just to get a breath," says Milton. "I do have several clients who have purchased inhalers from the street."

By all accounts, Detroit's inhaler black market remains small and underground, mostly consisting of individuals making person-to-person sales. Given the daunting barriers to accessing this life-saving medication legally, this black market plays a small but critical role for Detroit's most vulnerable asthmatics. However, even the black market does not fulfill all the medical needs of residents. "You have people out on the streets selling drugs, and we wish there were people selling inhalers," says Anderson.

Most inhalers are prescription medications, so sharing and selling them raises numerous issues. While few people (if any) have faced legal consequences from sharing or selling these medicines, there are legitimate medical concerns with using someone else's inhaler. Some, such as albuterol, are fast-acting rescue inhalers, suitable for treating asthma attacks. Others are slow-acting maintenance inhalers, designed to be used once or twice a day.

An uninformed buyer might end up relying on a maintenance inhaler during an asthma attack, with potentially tragic results, or might be using a rescue inhaler daily, which would do little for asthma prevention. Even if buyers know what kind of inhaler they're getting, the varying strengths and dosages may result in over-treating or under-treating, putting an increased burden on both patients and physicians.

Uncertainty over the amount of medicine black market buyers are getting is another pitfall. "Most asthmatics don't want to walk around with a few puffs in an expiring inhaler," says Lockridge.

According to residents, government at all levels has been slow to address the problem, even in areas such as Detroit's 48217 zip code - the most polluted one in the state. The neighborhood got its first MDEQ air monitoring station just last year. "I wonder why the state of Michigan hasn't done more to protect that community," says Milton. "They've really been a friend of business." Even though the area is in non-attainment for sulfur dioxide, in 2015, the MDEQ was poised to approve a request by the Marathon refinery to increase sulfur dioxide emissions.

Although activists successfully pressured MDEQ to make Marathon reduce emissions, the episode left a bitter taste in the mouths of many residents, and not many are optimistic that change is coming. Anderson puts it bluntly: "I think it's going to be business as usual."

For Detroit's asthmatics, "business as usual" would mean a continuation of a grim status quo - as long as the pollutants keep coming out of the smokestacks, then asthma, inhaler sharing, black markets, and uncertainty will continue to be a major part of their lives.

# What We Learn from the Mouse

by Deirdre McGovern

*From Anthrbio 368: Primate Social Behavior*

Nominated by Andrew Bernard

Deirdre writes with an engaging flair that far surpasses the scientific curve. Concurrently, she keeps to a tight organizational structure that indicates strong clarity of thought and attention to detail. Beyond her accurate account of many aspects of lemur behavior, Deirdre's descriptive treatments are interconnected to a degree that surpass expectations for this assignment. Within the inquiry portion of the paper, she tackles the question of seasonal torpor display in lemurs. Torpor is a rare behavior within the Primate order, and an interesting paper will question the evolutionary drivers of this behavior and why lemurs are uniquely situated to benefit from it. Deirdre, however, digs even deeper and probes how torpor tendencies vary by individual. Even more remarkable is her ability to address the two alternative hypotheses within a behavioral framework that drove home the class themes of reproductive success and competition. This was a pleasure to read, and I anticipate drawing from Deirdre's work to inspire my own research into the relationship between primates and their environment.

*Andrew Bernard*

# What We Learn from the Mouse

## Introduction

Too often we view human intelligence as the singularity which separates, and to an extent isolates, us from the rest of the natural world. Yet, delving into non-human primates reveals behavioral sophistication that astounds those who forget our closest genetic links. Even when considering some of the most ancient primates, the lemurs, one can find nuanced networks of social relationships, communication, and choice that challenge that which we believe distinguishes us as humans. How does a primate that weighs just 60 grams, or about six sharpie markers, recognize and build matrilineal relationships? How can it sustain periods of complete inactivity—near hibernation—when resources are scarce? There is an old fable about a lion and a mouse, in which the larger, more powerful lion vastly underestimates the value of the mouse. For those who know the end of the fable, the lion has made a mistake. The abilities of our closest living relatives raise questions of our own human capabilities. Examining behaviors of primates, such as the Grey mouse lemur (*Microcebus murinus*), may unlock complexities in our own species.

## Taxonomy

On the island of Madagascar off Africa's mainland lives a robust, small primate threatened with decline. The Grey mouse lemur, of the order Primate and the suborder Strepsirrhini, makes its home along with all other members of the infraorder Lemuriformes. Further distinguished under the family of Cheirogaleidae, or dwarf lemurs, *M. murinus* is among the smallest, but hardiest, of all primates in the world.

## Spacing and Diet

An important component of the Grey mouse lemur's resilience is its diet, which is intrinsically linked to its spatial patterns. Setash and colleagues (2017) note that Grey mouse lemurs are found in primary and secondary dry deciduous forests along Madagascar's western half. Typically, lower population densities of *M. murinus* are found in secondary dry deciduous forests than in primary dry deciduous forests (Ganzhorn and Schmid, 1998), but population densities from a meta-analysis (Setash, *et al.*, 2017) predict that the average population density for *M. murinus* is 0.9 per hectare, which is higher than many other estimated *Microcebus* densities. The data suggests that adaptations of Grey mouse lemurs allow them to better utilize space than other *Microcebus* species.

*M. murinus* is a nocturnal, solitary primate that spends its nights foraging for food. Wimmer, Tautz, and Kappeler (2002) found through an extensive summary of the literature that the home range patters of Grey mouse lemurs vary spatially and by sex-ratio across Madagascar, but that the majority of female home ranges have a degree of overlap and are nested within male ranges. A comparison to other *Microcebus* species found that *M. murinus* have relatively smaller females home ranges. This decrease in spacing is directly related to their diet (Dammhahn & Kappeler, 2009b).

Grey mouse lemurs consume insects (arthropods), insect secretions, small vertebrates, nectar, fruit, and gum—an ample diet that varies seasonally (Dammhahn & Kappeler, 2008). During times of food scarcity, typical of Madagascar's dry season, Grey mouse lemurs will feed on gum and honeydew. During the wet season, when food is plentiful, they are more likely to consume sugar-rich nectar (Joly-Radko & Zimmermann, 2010).

*M. murinus'* anatomical features are well adapted to their diet of invertebrates and vertebrates. Toussaint *et al.* (2015) found within a laboratory setting that *M. murinus* uses grasping, a common behavior in primates, not only to navigate fine branches, but also to capture live prey. Their ability to visually locate movement and then direct their grasp lends itself to targeting protein-rich live prey.

When considering the effect of their diet on their relatively reduced home-range sizes, Dammhahn and Kappeler (2009a) found that the overall diversity and wide distribution of their food sources reduces competition between individuals, leading *M. murinus* females to cluster their ranges closely around food resources. Thorén *et al.* (2011) echoed these same findings when comparing the Grey mouse lemur to another sympatric species of mouse lemur. The variety within *M. murinus'* diet reduces female competition for resources leading to smaller female home ranges and higher association with other neighboring females (Dammhahn & Kappeler, 2009b).

## Exploring the Mating System

Grey mouse lemur's reproduction strategy further demonstrates the intricacies of solitary primates' mating systems. Brevity is a major influence on their mating strategies, as both *M. murinus'* mating season and female estrous period are relatively short. Grey mouse lemurs mate seasonally, which is unusual across both Strepsirrhines and Haplorrhines. On average, females enter estrous only for brief periods after torpor, limiting the mating season to around four weeks (Eberle & Kappeler, 2002). Within that window, female Grey mouse lemurs are only sexually receptive for *one night* of each estrous cycle (Eberle & Kappeler, 2004a). As Grey mouse lemurs are solitary, sexually receptive females are dispersed spatially and temporally across the four weeks of the mating season. These factors combine with a typical primate population structure—overlapping male and female home ranges—to form a promiscuous mating system (Andrès & Solignac, 2003) characterized by both contest and scramble competition (Eberle & Kappeler, 2004b). Contest competition arises when a male monopolizes a female—limiting access to her by excluding others. Females, in response, use countermeasures to ensure they mate with multiple males, making matings an accessible resource for all individuals leading to scramble competition.

Because females are solitary, male monopolization of multiple receptive females is difficult if not impossible (Eberle & Kappeler, 2004b). As a consequence, male Gray mouse lemurs' mating strategies are varied and influenced by the proximity of both receptive females and competing males within their territories.

This limits each individual male's ability to mate guard, leading to alternative strategies such as excluding other males from territory—where body size is an influencing factor—and roaming for mates. (Eberle & Kappeler, 2002). Eberle & Kappeler (2004b) found that males who choose to roam and have high mate-finding abilities, or were able to win contests over other males, had the highest mating success.

Sperm competition also plays a vital role in *M. murinus*' mating system, as larger males typically sire more offspring, even when females are mating multiple males. Findings suggest that volume of sperm is critical within this promiscuous system (Eberle & Kappeler, 2004a). Grey mouse lemurs have relatively large testes for their body size (Eberle & Kappeler, 2002) which indicates the importance of sperm competition. Yet, testes size isn't everything. Timing of copulation is also key. From controlled experiments, Eberle, *et al.* (2007) found that males who inseminated females earlier in their receptive period—but not necessarily first—were most likely to sire her subsequent offspring. Their findings were supported by implications that many roaming males seek matings earlier within female's receptive period and are more likely to mate guard a female when she is first receptive (Eberle, Perret, & Kappeler, 2007).

Female mating strategies prove to be just as intricate. Female *M. murinus* work actively against male sexual monopolization by allowing both multiple mates and multiple copulations by those mates. In doing so, females ensure both genetic diversity among their offspring and greater potential for obtaining high-quality genetic material (Eberle & Kappeler, 2004a). Captive studies have demonstrated that female Grey mouse lemurs will direct aggression toward some males' solicitations, signifying mate choice (Andrès & Solignac, 2003). Females also exhibit mate choice, particularly in contest competition, by preferring males who have won more contests. Females did not show a preference toward any specific male body weight (Gomez *et al.*, 2011), which offers an interesting role-reversal to sexual dimorphism. Although typically monomorphic, *M. murinus* experiences seasonally-reversed sexual dimorphism, meaning that females begin to weigh more than males as they prepare for gestation (Eberle & Kappeler, 2002).

The diversity of interactions demonstrates the complexity of the Grey mouse lemur mating system. When looking at the impact of both male and female mating strategies and their outcomes, one must consider that many *M. murinus* litters have mixed paternities (Eberle & Kappeler, 2004b). It seems that females seek genetic diversity and monopolization avoidance by mating multiple mates, while males seek either single, guarded matings or many, roaming matings. The outcome of the litters suggests that more often than not, females successfully achieve diverse paternal genetic investment. Gomez and colleagues (2011) concluded that their findings supported flexible sex-roles within Grey mouse lemurs where both males and females demonstrated mate choice.

**Grouping Patterns and Kinship**

Like most Strepsirrhines, the solitary Grey mouse lemur does not form groups with conspecifics. Although there is home range overlap, their lack of shared home ranges is likely driven by food scarcity during the dry season, lack of female association during foraging, and their genetic link to a solitary ancestor. Yet, shared genetics and complex kin relationships influence many interactions within these primates' daily lives. Although solitary and foraging for food sources alone at night, during the day females will share nesting sites. Territories are often clustered around a well-established food sources, and nesting sites are usually found on these shared, overlapping home ranges. Wimmer, Tautz, and Kappeler (2002) found that the vast majority of females who share overlapping home ranges and sleeping hollows are related. Kin-recognition must be an ability of Grey mouse lemurs as these related populations experience few instances of inbreeding.

Eberle and Kappeler (2006) supported these findings by recording behaviors within shared tree hollows, finding that female Grey mouse lemurs nest overnight with close maternal relatives. Their findings also demonstrated sophisticated kin-recognition, where females can discriminate between their own young and the young of other females, as witnessed through the transportation of only their own offspring from site to site during foraging. In addition to their ability to discriminate their own offspring, females will groom and nurse related offspring within tree hollows. There have even been recorded instances of females adopting related kin whose mother has died (Eberle & Kappeler, 2006). These cooperative rearing behaviors are dependent on shared, matrilineal genes.

Beyond shared space, Kessler and colleagues (2014) found that mothers' vocalizations during offspring socialization build lasting relationships and kin-recognition. Fixed, matrilineal vocal markers help individuals of the same matriline identify kin. Their findings concluded that a combination of genetic vocal signatures as well as a shared social environment during development contribute to matrilineal vocalizations that aid in kin-recognition (Kessler, *et al.*, 2014). These vocalizations are thought to drive much of female kin-correlated behaviors.

Kessler and colleagues (2012) also found evidence that there are genetic signatures in the vocalizations of patrilines as well, which could be used to avoid inbreeding. Females respond less to advertisement calls of patrilineal males than advertisement calls of unrelated males. Their findings suggest that Grey mouse lemurs' advertisement calls are an integral part of social structures for these solitary foragers and convey important lineage information (Kessler, Scheumann, Nash, & Zimmermann, 2012). Whether these vocal signatures, matrilineal and patrilineal, are genetically driven or develop through shared spaces during early development, they represent a complex network of kin-correlated behaviors that drive spatial organization for *M. murinus*.

## Social Relationships and Dispersal

The social relationships of Grey mouse lemurs further add to a sophistication one would not expect from a solitary primate and expand on kin-correlated behaviors. Daily interactions reveal a stronger influence of female-female sociality than male-female or male-male sociality. Maternal bonds and relatedness lead to the formation of related female 'neighborhoods' centered around sleeping sites.

Lack of related male-female and male-male sociality is predominantly attributed to male-biased dispersal. Schliehe-Diecks and colleagues (2012) found that male Grey mouse lemurs will begin transitioning to a new range right before adulthood. They spend approximately two weeks making direct movements away from and then returning to their natal sites. This process is thought to be the necessary precursor to dispersal. During this transitional period, Schliehe-Diecks and colleagues (2012) surmise that the male collects resource information away from his natal site (about 180 and 960 meters, or between 1-7 home range diameters) and then returns back to his natal territory to ensure energetic costs are met by a familiar environment. After the transitional period, the male will transfer completely to a new territory and not return to his natal site (Schliehe-Diecks *et al.*, 2012). Due to this, many males no longer share overlapping ranges with close kin with whom they were socialized and thus rarely form sleeping groups of any kind. They usually sleeping solitarily or, at most, in pairs (Wimmer *et al.*, 2002).

Males will also typically disperse before the mating season, and Radespiel and colleagues (2003) found that the probability of inbreeding is low for mother-son dyads (3.8%) and slightly higher for father-daughter dyads (21.0%). The increased probability for inbreeding in father-daughter dyads can be attributed to female and adult males' lack of dispersal, leading to a higher probability of fathers and daughters inhabiting close home ranges during mating seasons. As adolescent males disperse, particularly before mating season, Radespiel and colleagues (2003) attribute the behavior to mother-son inbreeding avoidance.

Despite the probability of inbreeding, genomic analysis shows a lack of inbreeding which suggests that male dispersal results in high levels of gene flow between more stable female groups (Wimmer *et al.*, 2002). The potential for inbreeding increases as degree of relation decreases though, particularly for closely related male-female dyads (41.7%). However, using ten generations of wild Grey mouse lemurs, Huchard and colleges (2016) determined that male-biased dispersal and mate-choice are significant factors for lack of inbreeding. Male and female *M. murinus*, despite having a relatively high probability for inbreeding, seem to select mates that share less genetic relatedness using a mechanism not fully understood (Huchard, *et al.*, 2016). These tactics result in low occurrences of inbreeding and lack of inbreeding depression in genetics.

Low sociality between males and females can be partially explained by male dispersal, which separates related males and females who were socialized together. Yet, Schliehe-Diecks and colleagues (2012) note that not all males disperse. Lack of sociality between males and females can also be explained by female Grey mouse lemurs who, like many other Malagasy lemurs, are dominant over males (Hohenbrink, *et al.*, 2016). Observations of *M. murinus* in captivity have shown that females exhibit more territorial behaviors (i.e. rubbing and urine-marking) compared to males as they reach between 8-9 months of age. Play behaviors witnessed in juveniles of both sexes evolves into female intolerance and dominance over males within a year of birth (Hohenbrink *et al.*, 2015). In the wild, observations support these findings and show that adult females win the majority of conflicts over males regardless of location and season (Hohenbrink *et al.*, 2016). Due to their social organization, male and female Grey mouse lemurs do not form social relationships.

## Torpor and Who It Benefits

A final component of the Grey mouse lemur's behavior, torpor, has been touched upon in passing in previous sections; however, the broader implications of torpor are somewhat perplexing. Torpor is interwoven with all aspects of the Grey mouse lemur's life history. By definition, torpor is a daily period of inactivity intended to save energy. It is commonly witnessed in Grey mouse lemurs during the times of low resource availability in Madagascar's dry season (Biggar *et al.*, 2015b). Madagascar's dry season is characterized by both low resource availability and low temperatures (Schmid, 1999) which can prove to be a fatal period for individuals unable to adapt to changing temperatures. Grey mouse lemur's ability to enter torpor stems from their classification at heterotherms—species that can change their metabolic rates as an energy-saving strategy in adverse environments.

Among the primates, heterothermy is found in Cheirogaleidae family, which includes Grey mouse lemurs (Dausmann, 2014), but is thought to be a shared, ancestral trait in all primates (Biggar *et al.*, 2015a). While heterotherms can change their metabolic rates as a way to decrease energetic needs in time of resource scarcity, extensive research still has not fully illuminated why there are variation in individuals' use of torpor (Vuarin *et al.*, 2013). A comprehensive framework is needed to understand the basic questions: who employs torpor and why?

*M. murinus*' torpor can be explained by shifts in gene activation responsible for achieving and maintaining a period of inactivity. Biggar and colleagues (2015b) found that multi-gene and multi-organ metabolic changes are necessary in sustaining torpor; however, the genetic complexity is much less than that required for hibernation in other species. Grey mouse lemurs also have specific anatomical adaptions for torpor, such as the ability to lower their body temperature without shivering (an energetically costly behavior) and the ability to use body lipids as energy during torpor (Biggar *et al.*, 2015a). Although the exact mechanism for how torpor is first implemented is still unclear, these anatomical findings help explain how Grey mouse lemurs can achieve and maintain torpor.

There are two hypotheses for how Grey mouse lemurs implement torpor, which stem from the knowledge that heterothermy is both flexible and individual-dependent, but also seasonally regulated (Dausmann, 2014). First, the *anticipatory cues hypothesis* suggests that environmental factors associated with the transition from the wet season to the dry season (i.e. lower temperatures) signal individuals to start using torpor. Second, the *food shortage hypothesis* states that torpor results from individual's sensitivity to changes in food availability (Vuarin, *et al.*, 2015). These hypotheses have been investigated in the field, and Vuarin and colleagues (2015) found that Grey mouse lemurs in the wild, if given a supplemental diet, would postpone torpor by 1-2 months and retain a higher skin temperatures than individuals not on the supplemental diet. Their findings suggest that torpor is triggered by internal mechanisms adjusted to reduced environmental resources (Vuarin *et al.*, 2015). However, Vuarin and Henry (2014) concluded that food shortage alone is not a comprehensive explanation for torpor. One must consider confounding factors, such as resource conversion into body fat, nutritional composition of available food, and shortage of water.

These findings ask an even larger question by suggesting that Grey mouse lemurs are evaluating their environment and on some level choosing when or if to enter torpor. While one cannot assert that Grey mouse lemurs consciously choose whether or not to enter torpor, an internal mechanism of some sophistication is clearly driving their changes in metabolic state. This makes torpor both an ability and a choice. With the consideration of individual choice and torpor, there are equally perplexing observations that suggest some individuals cannot enter torpor—even when it is beneficial to their survival. The reasons for this inability are also largely unknown (Faherty et al., 2016). Torpor affects every behavior from the initiation of the mating season to resiliency to deforestation. On a fundamental level, it would seem that torpor is essential to surviving the resource-scarce dry season, and that torpor should be a beneficial energy-saving strategy deployed by all individuals. Yet, there is variation in who can and will enter torpor, and, ultimately, one has to ask: which individuals benefit the most from torpor?

Research findings suggest that factors such as size, age, and sex are constantly interacting to determine whether a specific individual will enter torpor or not. Age and seasonal changes in body weight (i.e. weight gain during the rainy season) are significant factors that affect a Grey mouse lemur's ability to enter and sustain torpor (Vuarin et al., 2013). Faherty and colleagues (2016) found that individuals who were heavier and larger tended to enter deeper torpor states than smaller, leaner individuals. As Grey mouse lemurs are prominently monomorphic during dry seasons, or similarly sized regardless of sex, one has to consider the intersection of sex and size. Schmid (1999) found evidence of striking sex-based differences in survival mechanisms during Madagascar's dry season. Doing mark-and-recapture studies during the dry season, Schmid (1999) noted that while only 18.9% of males stayed inactive during the four to five-month dry season, 73.1% of females were inactive. This study suggests that there are two sex-specific survival mechanisms for the dry season: the majority of males will remain active but partake in torpors of less than twenty-four hours. Females will remain inactive for days to several weeks, and thus experience a fattening period before the start of the dry season and ultimately lose up to 31.7% of their body weight. At the end of the dry season, there is no difference in mass and tail circumference between males and females (Schmid, 1999). These findings coincide with Faherty and colleagues (2016) findings that size is a positive factor for torpor length, and suggest that females, particularly those who have undergone a fattening period, should be the most likely to utilize torpor.

The advantage of torpor to females is further confirmed when considering the potential hazards of not entering torpor. Torpor, paradoxically, can be both a beneficial energy-saving strategy and extremely energetically costly. Landes and colleagues (2017) examined these costs in a laboratory setting and found that by artificially inducing another season (and thus another metabolic change) into the Grey mouse lemur's yearly cycle, an individual's chances of dying increased three or four-fold. Grey mouse lemur's ability to metabolically adjust to the temperatures of a changing environment in the wild is essential to torpor as ambient temperatures in Madagascar drop during the dry season (Terrien *et al.*, 2010). Behavioral thermoregulation, or behaviors that help individuals maintain a desired body temperature, include actions such as seeking a more sheltered, thus warmer, nesting site (Terrien *et al.*, 2010). Terrien and colleagues (2010) found that females engaged in more thermoregulatory behaviors than males did, but that as age increased, so too did thermoregulatory behaviors regardless of sex. Their findings implicate that as Grey mouse lemurs age, they have less tolerance for colder ambient temperatures and changes in body temperature. They also suggest that females are overall less tolerant to colder temperatures and should seek periods of inactivity more frequently than males, who are more tolerant of being active even in lowered temperatures.

Age and sex were also found to have an effect on seasonal stress, with females showing markedly more stress in response to seasonal changes in environment as they age, exhibiting higher levels of glucocorticoids (Hämäläinen, *et al.*, 2015). This study also posited that this increase in stress was due to the anticipated energetic costs of reproducing and gestating after the dry season (Hämäläinen, *et al.*, 2015).

These findings touch upon what seems to be a major biological drawback to torpor: periods of inactivity limit individuals' abilities to reproduce. However, the Grey mouse lemurs' ability to regulate metabolic stress associated with torpor on a cellular level allows them to live above-average lifespans compared to mammals of similar sizes. This increase in lifespan allows for each individual to partake in more seasonal mating periods than would be expected given their tendency for torpor (Blanco & Zehr, 2015). Within this above-average lifespan, females typically live longer than males (Hämäläinen, *et al.*, 2015), and therefore live through more mating seasons. Even with their increased glucocorticoid response to seasonal changes and the coming reproductive season, females experience less of a disadvantage by using torpor. As they live longer than males, they live through more reproductive periods.

Returning to the original question of who benefits from torpor especially when considering the potential consequences, one can see that females ultimately have the most to gain from torpor as an energy-saving strategy for both immediate resource scarcity and reproductive costs at the end of the dry season. Female *M. murinus*' benefits are also further explained when considering seasonally-based food shortages and the implications of torpor on the reduction of intraspecific food competition. Grey mouse lemurs exhibit some sympatry with closely related species of mouse lemurs, in particular *M. ravelobensis*. Reduction in *M. murinus* locomotion in the early stages of the dry season (often due to torpor) reduces food competition in shared food sources between these two species, perhaps alleviated the stress of resources-competition for those *M. murinus* individuals who are not exhibiting torpor (Thorén *et al.*, 2011).

Torpor ultimately proves to be a delicate balance between several variables, such as length of inactivity, age, body size, and sex. When these factors are balanced, they lead to an advantageous behavior for Grey mouse lemurs. This is seen particularly in healthy females, who have the most to gain from an energy-saving strategy against Madagascar's resource-scare dry season and imminent mating season.

## Conservation and the Question of Resiliency

Unlike many of the lemurs found on Madagascar, the Grey mouse lemur is categorized as 'Least Concern' under the International Union for the Conservation of Nature (IUCN). However, despite its current population levels, *M. murinus'* status is far from stable and most likely already in decline (IUCN, 2017).

According to the IUCN (2017), several factors threaten the Grey mouse lemur's historically ubiquitous populations. All of them are man-made. Agricultural practices, mining and quarrying, and intentional hunting and trapping of *M. murinus* are among its highest threats (IUCN, 2017). Various studies on different geographical regions of Madagascar further illustrate the multi-faceted threat to populations. In Madagascar's western regions, deforestation for slash-and-burn agricultural practices destroy primary dry deciduous forests. The practice threatens the Grey mouse lemur in particular by disrupting its torpor, which require specific nesting conditions. Secondary forests often provide less shelter, in the form of tree holes, and less protection against daily raising temperatures, thus rendering torpor impossible (Ganzhorn & Schmid 1998). Ganzhorn and Schmid (1998) concluded in their research more than two decades ago that survival rates of *M. murinus* in secondary dry deciduous forests are much lower than in primary dry deciduous forests.

The threats to the Grey mouse lemur are complex. For as easy as it is to demonize human practices that adversely affect wildlife, the populations who employ them are often also in need of resources. For as much as we threaten them, there are also many individuals who seek to protect and preserve *M. murinus*. Fortunately, the Grey mouse lemur is protected under current, international legislation, such as the Convention on International Trade in Endangered Species (CITES) Article I, which works to regulate and restrict the import and export of endangered species (CITES, 2017). Yet, the Lion and the Mouse fable has two endings: one where the Lion appreciates the Mouse and another where it eats the Mouse. Here we see that we are the Lion, and all the other biodiversity with whom we share this planet are the legions of proverbial Mice. We are at a crossroads for which ending to the fable we choose, and investing research in that which makes this species so unique might be the only solution to its conservation. Otherwise, as the story might continue, there will be no one to remove the thorns in our paw.

Grey mouse lemurs are a resilient and hardy species, found in many diverse habitats across Madagascar, including many protected forests and parks (IUCN, 2017). Current research by Sawyer and colleagues (2016) concludes that the Grey mouse lemur may prove more adaptive than previously thought due to its high terrestrial mobility, small body weight, and diverse, omnivorous diet. Sampling done in Northeastern Madagascar's Masoala Peninsula demonstrated that *M. murinus* was the most tolerant of the species studied to changing or degraded habitats (Sawyer *et al.*, 2016). Owing to their unique versatility and energy saving strategies, Grey mouse lemurs represent hope for the future of observation and conservation of primate species in the wild.

References

Andrès, M., & Solignac, M. (2003). Mating System in Mouse Lemurs: Theories and Facts, Using Analysis of Paternity. *Folia Primatologica, 74*(5-6), 355-366.

Biggar, K. K., Wu, C., Tessier, S. N., Zhang, J., Pifferi, F., Perret, M., & Storey, K. B. (2015a). Primate Torpor: Regulation of Stress-activated Protein Kinases During Daily Torpor in the Gray Mouse Lemur, Microcebus murinus. *Genomics, Proteomics & Bioinformatics, 13*(2), 81-90.

Biggar, K. K., Wu, C., Tessier, S. N., Zhang, J., Pifferi, F., Perret, M., & Storey, K. B. (2015b). Modulation of Gene Expression in Key Survival Pathways During Daily Torpor in the Gray Mouse Lemur, Microcebus murinus. *Genomics, Proteomics & Bioinformatics, 13*(2), 111-118.

Blanco, M. B., & Zehr, S. M. (2015). Striking longevity in a hibernating lemur. *Journal of Zoology, 296*(3), 177-188.

CITES. 2017. Retrieved at: https://cites.org/legislation.

Dammhahn, M., & Kappeler, P. M. (2008). Comparative Feeding Ecology of Sympatric Microcebus berthae and M. murinus. *International Journal of Primatology, 29*(6), 1567-1589.

Dammhahn, M., & Kappeler, P. M. (2009a). Females go where the food is: does the socio-ecological model explain variation in social organisation of solitary foragers? *Behavioral Ecology and Sociobiology, 63*(6), 939-952.

Dammhahn, M., & Kappeler, P. M. (2009b). Scramble or contest competition over food in solitarily foraging mouse lemurs (Microcebus spp.): New insights from stable isotopes. *American Journal of Physical Anthropology, 141*(2), 181-189.

Dausmann, K. H. (2014). Flexible patterns in energy savings: heterothermy in primates. Journal of Zoology, 292(2), 101-111.

Eberle, M., & Kappeler, P. M. (2002). Mouse lemurs in space and time: a test of the socioecological model. *Behavioral Ecology and Sociobiology, 51*(2), 131-139.

Eberle, M., & Kappeler, P. M. (2004a). Selected polyandry: female choice and inter-sexual conflict in a small nocturnal solitary primate (Microcebus murinus). *Behavioral Ecology and Sociobiology, 57*(1), 91-100.

Eberle, M., & Kappeler, P. M. (2004b). Sex in the dark: determinants and consequences of mixed male mating tactics in Microcebus murinus, a small solitary nocturnal primate. *Behavioral Ecology and Sociobiology, 57*(1), 77-90.

Eberle, M., & Kappeler, P. M. (2006). Family insurance: kin selection and cooperative breeding in a solitary primate (Microcebus murinus). *Behavioral Ecology and Sociobiology, 60*(4), 582-588.

Eberle, M., Perret, M., & Kappeler, P. M. (2007). Sperm Competition and Optimal Timing of Matings in Microcebus murinus. *International Journal of Primatology, 28*(6), 1267-1278.

Faherty, S. L., Campbell, C. R., Hilbig, S. A., & Yoder, A. D. (2016). The effect of body mass and diet composition on torpor patterns in a Malagasy primate (Microcebus murinus). *Journal of Comparative Physiology B, 187*(4), 677-688.

Ganzhorn, J.U. & Schmid, J. (1998). Different Population Dynamics of Microcebus murinus in Primary and Secondary Deciduous Dry Forests of Madagascar. *International Journal of Primatology, 19*(5), 785-796.

Gomez, D., Huchard, E., Henry, P., & Perret, M. (2011). Mutual mate choice in a female-dominant and sexually monomorphic primate. *American Journal of Physical Anthropology, 147*(3), 370-379.

Hämäläinen, A., Heistermann, M., & Kraus, C. (2015). The stress of growing old: sex- and season-specific effects of age on allostatic load in wild grey mouse lemurs. *Oecologia, 178*(4), 1063-1075.

Hohenbrink, S., Koberstein-Schwarz, M., Zimmermann, E., & Radespiel, U. (2015). Shades of gray mouse lemurs: Ontogeny of female dominance and dominance-related behaviors in a nocturnal primate. *American Journal of Primatology, 77*(11), 1158-1169.

Hohenbrink, S., Schaarschmidt, F., Bünemann, K., Gerberding, S., Zimmermann, E., & Radespiel, U. (2016). Female dominance in two basal primates, Microcebus murinus and Microcebus lehilahytsara: variation and determinants. *Animal Behaviour, 122*, 145-156.

Huchard, E., Schliehe-Diecks, S., Kappeler, P. M., & Kraus, C. (2016). The inbreeding strategy of a solitary primate, Microcebus murinus. *Journal of Evolutionary Biology, 30*(1), 128-140.

IUCN. 2017. *The IUCN Red List of Threatened Species – Microcebus murinus.* Retrieved at: www.iucnredlist.org/details/biblio/13323/0.

Joly-Radko, M., & Zimmermann, E. (2010). Seasonality in Gum and Honeydew Feeding in Gray Mouse Lemurs. *The Evolution of Exudativory in Primates*, 141-153.

Kessler, S. E., Radespiel, U., Hasiniaina, A. I., Leliveld, L. M., Nash, L. T., & Zimmermann, E. (2014). Modeling the origins of mammalian sociality: moderate evidence for matrilineal signatures in mouse lemur vocalizations. *Frontiers in Zoology, 11*(1), 14.

Kessler, S. E., Scheumann, M., Nash, L. T., & Zimmermann, E. (2012). Paternal kin recognition in the high frequency / ultrasonic range in a solitary foraging mammal. *BMC Ecology, 12*(1), 26.

Landes, J., Perret, M., Hardy, I., Camarda, C. G., Henry, P., & Pavard, S. (2017). State transitions: a major mortality risk for seasonal species. *Ecology Letters, 20*(7), 883-891.

Radespiel, U., Lutermann, H., Schmelting, B., Bruford, M. W., & Zimmermann, E. (2003). Patterns and dynamics of sex-biased dispersal in a nocturnal primate, the grey mouse lemur, Microcebus murinus. *Animal Behaviour, 65*(4), 709-719.

Sawyer, R. M., Fenosoa, Z. S., Andrianarimisa, A., & Donati, G. (2016). The effect of habitat disturbance on the abundance of nocturnal lemur species on the Masoala Peninsula, northeastern Madagascar. *Primates, 58*(1), 187-197.

Schliehe-Diecks, S., Eberle, M., & Kappeler, P. M. (2012). Walk the line— dispersal movements of gray mouse lemurs (Microcebus murinus). *Behavioral Ecology and Sociobiology, 66*(8), 1175-1185.

Schmid, J. (1999). Sex-Specific Differences in Activity Patterns and Fattening in the Gray Mouse Lemur (Microcebus murinus) in Madagascar. *Journal of Mammalogy, 80*(3), 749-757.

Setash, C. M., Zohdy, S., Gerber, B. D., & Karanewsky, C. J. (2017). A biogeographical perspective on the variation in mouse lemur density throughout Madagascar. *Mammal Review, 47*(3), 212-229.

Terrien, J., Perret, M., & Aujard, F. (2010). Gender markedly modulates behavioral thermoregulation in a non-human primate species, the mouse lemur (Microcebus murinus). *Physiology & Behavior, 101*(4), 469-473.

Thorén, S., Quietzsch, F., Schwochow, D., Sehen, L., Meusel, C., Meares, K., & Radespiel, U. (2011). Seasonal Changes in Feeding Ecology and Activity Patterns of Two Sympatric Mouse Lemur Species, the Gray Mouse Lemur (Microcebus murinus) and the Golden-brown Mouse Lemur (M. ravelobensis), in Northwestern Madagascar. *International Journal of Primatology, 32*(3), 566-586.

Toussaint, S., Herrel, A., Ross, C. F., Aujard, F., & Pouydebat, E. (2015). Substrate Diameter and Orientation in the Context of Food Type in the Gray Mouse Lemur, Microcebus murinus: Implications for the Origins of Grasping in Primates. *International Journal of Primatology, 36*(3), 583-604.

Vuarin, P., Dammhahn, M., & Henry, P. (2013). Individual flexibility in energy saving: body size and condition constrain torpor use. *Functional Ecology, 27*(3), 793-799.

Vuarin, P., Dammhahn, M., Kappeler, P. M., & Henry, P. (2015). When to initiate torpor use? Food availability times the transition to winter phenotype in a tropical heterotherm. *Oecologia, 179*(1), 43-53.

Vuarin, P., & Henry, P. (2014). Field evidence for a proximate role of food shortage in the regulation of hibernation and daily torpor: a review. *Journal of Comparative Physiology B, 184*(6), 683-697.

Wimmer, B., Tautz, D., & Kappeler, P. M. (2002). The genetic population structure of the gray mouse lemur (Microcebus murinus), a basal primate from Madagascar. *Behavioral Ecology and Sociobiology, 52*, 166-175.

# Winning Essays
## Granader Prize for Excellence in Upper-Level Writing (social sciences)

## Modern Sports as Pre-Modern in Media
by Jessica Baer
*From PolSci 368: Sports, Politics, and Society*
Nominated by Emma Waitzman (GSI), Andrei Markovits (Faculty)

In this essay, Jessica takes a creative approach to addressing how concepts of modernity manifest in sports. By using the movie "Fever Pitch," Jessica provides an accessible and entertaining example to untangle complicated sociological concepts. She uncovers American's desire to hold onto pre-modern aspects of sports in the face of an ever-modernizing world. What is particularly special about this essay is Jessica's thorough research. She expertly bridges the gap between film studies and sports, while being wary to not overshadow the core issue of paper with outside information. Additionally, in one paragraph, Jessica adds a personal dimension to the essay by thoughtfully drawing on her own experience. Simply put, Jessica's passion for the topic shines through. The essay is engaging and enlightening from start to finish.

*Emma Waitzman*

# Modern Sports as Pre-Modern in Media

Baseball is constantly classified as "America's favorite pastime." However, as the sport has gotten older, many aspects of experiencing a Major League Baseball (MLB) game have been modernized. The games are played in high-tech stadiums full of high-end restaurants, bars, and even night clubs. One could also flip through television channels and find countless baseball games being televised. Additionally, as baseball has developed, fans, sports networks, and the MLB have established a substantial dependence on statistical records. Each game contains thousands of quantifiable actions, such as RBIs, batting averages, earned run averages, pitching speed, stolen bases, and countless more. However, while sport has evolved to become more modern, film and television continue to romanticize and emphasize the pre-modernity of sport. Media does this because these aspects of the game are the reasons for fans' devotion to their teams; these followers would attend the games even if the modern aspects were removed. Though baseball in particular has heavily modernized through its maturation, several relatively modern baseball movies such as *Fever Pitch* (2005) challenge the modern aspects of the sport; movies such as this illustrate pre-modernity by showing fans' disregard of achievement, exemplifying a religious rather than secular focus of attending, and displaying elements of a collective-centralized mindset rather than one that is self-interested.

Many sport movies that center on baseball focus especially on the pre-modern aspects of the sport. Movies are an important indicator of fans' affectivity because of what they represent. As stated in Hortense Powdermaker's article "An Anthropologist looks at the movies," "Movies... functioning primarily on the emotional level through their production of daydreams...they are a form of art – that of telling a story...with tales of the conflicts between men and the resolution of the conflicts, with man's unfulfilled wishes and their fulfillment."[1] Movies allow

---

[1] Powdermaker, Hortense. "An Anthropologist Looks at the Movies." *The Annals of the American Academy of Political and Social Science*, vol. 254, 1947, pp. 80–87. *JSTOR*, JSTOR, www.jstor.org/stable/1026143.

us to enter a universe both parallel and completely more magical than our own, which draws us to them; they depict our culture, true desires, and fantasies. This essay discusses the movie *Fever Pitch*, which centers on Ben, a schoolteacher and devoted Red Sox fan from the age of seven. Throughout the movie, the Red Sox's 2004 season parallels Ben's courtship of Lindsey, an executive at a technology company. The peaks and slumps of the athletic season align with the passionately positive or devastating moments of the characters' relationship. Toward the end of the movie, the pair end the relationship, leading Ben to almost sell his lifetime season tickets. When Lindsey gets word that Ben is selling the tickets, she races to Fenway Park and is forced to run across the field to tell him he should not sell them. Consequently, the couple reunites and ultimately attends every game of the World Series that year, including the final game in which the Red Sox win.

Ben's commitment to attending every home game in *Fever Pitch* represents baseball fans' lack of care for their team's achievement, achievement being a modern classification. While pre-modernity focuses on the ascription-based aspects of human beings, such as family, race, religion, or ethnicity, this measurement has transformed over time into a modern, achievement-based evaluation. Talcott Parsons' "Pattern Variables" essay further elucidates this contrast: "ascription refers to qualities… or characteristics… achievement refers to performance, and emphasizes individual achievement."[2] The Red Sox lose very often, with some of the worst error inducing losses in history, yet Ben goes to every home game knowing they will probably lose. Ben exclaims, "That's right. I mean - why? Because they haven't won a World Series in a century or so? *So what?*" [italics added] This expresses the extent to which Ben disregards the achievement aspects of the game and more so cares about the personal qualities of attending the game. Ben loves the ambiance of the stadium, the scents, the feel of the seats, the sounds, as do the other fans around him. He is not merely there to see who wins

[2] Parsons, Talcott. "Pattern Variables Revisited: A Response to Robert Dubin." *American Sociological Review*, vol. 25, no. 4, 1960, doi:10.2307/2092932.

or loses the game, but for everything that accompanies experiencing the game. As ascription aligns with pre-modernity because it focuses on characteristics rather than statistics, Ben embodies a fan's focus on qualities of the game that have nothing to do with the team's achievement or the game's final score. Rather, devoted fans such as Ben attend the game for qualitative reasons.

In conjunction with fans' desires for the qualitative aspects of the game, fans also challenge modernity by attending games because of the collectivity aspect of baseball rather than for self-interests. Collectivism is an emphasis on a group mentality rather than on individual priority. Harry C. Triandis explains, "Collectivists are closely linked individuals who view themselves primarily as parts of a whole, be it a family, a network of co-workers, a tribe, or a nation."[3] Furthering this point concerning sport, Allen Guttmann writes, "baseball [is] associated with…'The American sounds of summer, the tap of bat against ball, the cries of the infielders, the wooden plump of the ball into catchers' mitts'… baseball was indeed 'the summer game.'"[4] Baseball embodies an entire season every year: baseball is summer, and summer is baseball. More so, Guttmann includes the adjective "American" to define baseball's embodiment of the sounds of summer. This indicates the nationalistic collective mindset behind attending a game; a patriotic aspect linked to being part of a whole. Going to a baseball game allows spectators to feel the American collectivity of ringing in summer together.

Sports media, such as *Fever Pitch*, perpetuate and emphasize this phenomenon. In the movie, Ben states, "They're here. Every April, they're here. At 1:05 or at 7:05, there is a game. And if it gets rained out, guess what? They make it up to you. Does anyone else in your life do that? The Red Sox don't get divorced. This is a real family. This is the family that's here for you." Ben goes to the games for the community and familial aspects, not to merely watch the players perform. A Huffington Post writer and major baseball fan, Michael Giltz, parallels Ben's

[3] Triandis, H. C. (1995). New directions in social psychology. *Individualism & collectivism*. Boulder, CO: Westview Press.
[4] Nixon, Howard L., and Allen Guttmann. "A Whole New Ball Game: An Interpretation of American Sports." *Contemporary Sociology*, vol. 18, no. 2, 1989, p. 269., doi:10.2307/2074124.

mentality as he writes, "First it was the excitement...But now it's...the chance to chat with lifelong friends I've made in the Bleacher Creature section."[5] This represents the collectivity and the shared interests of fans as opposed to the extent of self-interest associated with any action; this is a lack of egoism and interest in the collective, a focus on the whole. Ben is also attending these games in a particular section with a group that he considers his "summer family." A large reason he goes to these games is to experience the win or loss with these people, rather than watch the game at home alone. Allen Guttmann further comments on the mere enjoyment of experiencing the game by writing, "What is the goal of leapfrog other than the pleasures of leapfrog?"[6] Though leapfrog can be quantified by pitting teams against each other and scoring wins such as baseball can, the point of the games are not the quantifiable outcomes but the experience. The point of being at the game is that there is in fact no material point; fans attend for the pleasure of the experience, for the shared understanding and the comradery, not for any specific plays or outcomes.

The collective experience of attending a baseball game is further emphasized through the importance of baseball idioms in American culture. The shared understanding of these idioms is what unites not just fans, but Americans as a whole. Andrei S. Markovits lists dozens of idioms in *Offside: Soccer and American Exceptionalism*, such as "rain check," "hitting it out of the park," "it's a whole new ball game," "that's the ballgame," "striking out," "out of one's league,"[7] and many others. He comments on these idioms that, "the game [baseball]...so much part of American culture that many of its expressions entered the American vernacular, from which they have yet to disappear."[8] The fact that most everyone in America can understand these idioms, and that they have endured through

[5] Giltz, Michael. "Why I Love Baseball." *The Huffington Post*, TheHuffingtonPost.com, 8 Mar. 2011, www.huffingtonpost.com/entry/why-i-love-baseball_b_832733.html.

[6] Guttmann, Allen. "From Ritual to Record: A Retrospective Critique." *Sport History Review*, vol. 32, no. 1, 2001, pp. 2–11., doi:10.1123/shr.32.1.2.

[7] Markovits, Andrei S., Hellerman, Steven L., "The Formation of the American Sport Space "crowding out" and other factors in the relegation and marginalization of soccer."." *Offside*, doi:10.1515/9781400824182-004.

[8] Ibid.

baseball's modernization, indicates a group mentality of baseball that includes a tremendous amount of people. The importance and relevance of these idioms are also represented in *Fever Pitch*. When Ben meets Lindsey, he is touring her office with a group of students from his math class. One of the boys jokes with Ben that he is not of the caliber to date Lindsey, to which he responds "What? Wait. Are you saying that she's out of my league?" The student rebuts, "She is bringing some serious heat, man. I don't know if you got the bat speed." Ben finishes, "Oh, I got the bat speed. I got plenty of bat speed. I could hit her best cheese." This entire dialogue is based off baseball idioms. Though Ben is a devoted Red Sox fan and the student plays baseball at the school, the importance is that the movie viewer, too, understands this interaction. The American viewer comprehends what they are arguing over and can laugh about how the two go about arguing it. As exhibited, there is an emphasis on the pre-modern concept of the collective in baseball, rather than on the modern notion of self.

Furthermore, though sports have become more secular, their representation in media continues to reflect a pre-modern emphasis on religiosity. In older times, religion was a main part of daily life: people prayed for rain or harvest success, believed that gods were ruling over them, performed actions to please the gods, and overall included religion in their everyday choices. As the human race has developed over time, everyday events have, as a whole, become more secular. The government of America in particular has a tradition of "separation of church and state"[9] so as not to entangle the more emotional aspects of life with the more concrete legal-rational aspects of life. In the realm of sports, however, Markovits notes, "And yet, what gives the whole thing [sport] meaning is its pre-modernness – our delight, our fears, our associations, the quasi-religious experience: rituals,

---

[9] Reynolds v. United States, 98 U.S. 145 (1879); Mariana Servin-Gonzalez and Oscar Torres-Reyna, "The Polls-Trends: Religion and Politics," *Public Opinion Quarterly* 63 (Winter 1999): 592–621, 603.

chants, language, code, colors – it is a collective."[10] By this, Markovits is explaining that, though we might follow sport for several reasons, a primary motivation for attending a game is the "quasi-religious experience" of it. There are certain traditions of going to a game: donning particular clothing of specific colors, chanting "D-Fence" and other such expressions, saying the aforementioned idioms, singing songs such as "I'm shipping up to Boston" and, as shown in *Fever Pitch*, "Sweet Caroline." Attending a service at a religious institution follows many of these same guidelines. Church goers dress up in particular apparel when going to temple or church, sing songs, chant, speak in their own language. Moreover, both religious services and attending a baseball game involve comradery. I attend services at my temple on Yom Kippur and Rosh Hashanah mainly because friends and family are all coming together to share the experience with me, to sing the Shema together, speak Hebrew to one another, and catch up on each other's lives. Fans of baseball teams operate similarly in that spectators, though having a desire to sing and chant for their teams, enjoy most that they are singing and chanting with other fans. The collective aspect of religion is inherent in attending a baseball game.

Despite having many components that refute modernity, baseball does contain some aspects that are heavily modern. The most modern aspect of baseball is how quantified it has become. The statistics of baseball are a huge industry; even typing "Red Sox statistics" into google returns 15.2 million results in half a second. Gambling on these scores has also grown into a massive, all-consuming hobby for many people, where the focus is truly on the numbers. Some fans do, in fact, attend the games for the quantifiable aspects. However, this modern component of baseball is overshadowed by the pre-modern element of record keeping. Though record keeping could mistakenly be seen as purely modern,

---

[10] Markovits, Andrei. Sport Politics and Society. University of Michigan, Ann Arbor Michigan. September, 7 2017. Course Lecture.

records have always been kept as traditions. Stories of amazing feats and legendary events have been passed down through generations, and are, in fact, pre-modern. Merely because we can write and type all this information down now does not make our focus on history wholly modern. The focus for devoted fans is not on the numbers, but on the feats that the numbers represent. Our keeping of records merely signifies the modern maintenance of tales that has existed for centuries, in which legendary feats were remembered and retold orally.

Additionally, it could be argued that the global nature of baseball makes it entirely modern as a result of globalization. Though Red Sox baseball does contain a very centralized following, and Boston is saturated with an overwhelming Red Sox spirit, because of technology, Red Sox support is also global. People from all over the nation and all over the world care about Red Sox wins and losses[11] and can attend a game due to modernized travel. Industrialization and thus modernization has allowed anyone, at any time, anywhere with an internet connection, to turn on a baseball game. This is a modern aspect of sport. However, the Red Sox following, the Mets following, the Cubs following, the true passion for the game and for a team to succeed come not from those distantly watching, but from the local neighborhood surrounding those teams. This is exemplified by the much larger number of Red Sox fans in Massachusetts than anywhere else in the nation or the world.[12]

There is a strong, neighborhood-centralized, pre-modern motivation to support one's local team. In *Sport as a Major Cultural Construct*, Markovits explains, "In other words, these [1700s British ball games] were profoundly local phenomena unintelligible from village to village, let alone across the globe... These constructs [local derbies] then were, in the truest sense of the word, ad hoc events serving strictly local enjoyment."[13] Sports began as a local phenomenon

---

[11] "Map of Red Sox Nation." *Boston Red Sox*, MLB.com, 20 Jan. 2016, boston.redsox.mlb.com/bos/fan_forum/rsn_map.jsp.
[12] Ibid.
[13] Markovits, Andrei S. "Sport as a Major Cultural Construct in the Advanced Industrial World at the Beginning of the 21st Century: A Historical and Comparative Perspective." Vol. 4. Levi-Strauss-Museum Buttenheim, 2013.

that could not traverse boundaries as a result of rule variation. Yet, when sport modernized and governing organizations regularized rules, each village still developed independently in support of their local team; these tribal connections still exist today. In 2014, the New York Times published a density map of national MLB team support.[14] Though having a few dispersed spots, such as a patch of Yankee fans in Florida, where the article focuses on certain geographical lines, the stark contrast of team support is striking. The depiction of the Munson-Nixon Line, the precise demarcation between Red Sox and Yankee allegiances in New England, illustrates Connecticut's split. There is a clear division between a local Red Sox tribe and a Yankee allegiance. The Yankees take Hartford along with areas South and West of it, and the Eastern and Northern half of the state goes to the Sox. Though almost anyone from anywhere could attend a game, as the article depicts team support juxtaposed geographically, it is clear that local, tribal affiliations do, in fact, endure.

Moreover, this geographic dependence fosters a strong local team loyalty that is indicative of pre-modernity. Modern sports are a fundamental Kantian proposition[15] in that one truly has nothing to gain from a team's win or loss – a win does not astronomically improve one's life, while a loss does not tremendously regress one's life. Kant proposed that the only way to determine something's value is if no personal gain will result. Sport attachment is precisely such a compact; most of us are rabid fans for no particular gain and are in fact attached to something that fails often. This loyalty is the primary focus of *Fever Pitch* in that Ben feels he has a strong commitment to the Sox even though the team does not know he exists, the outcome of the game has nothing to do with him attending, and they lose more than they win. Ben is so invested in the Sox that even when attending the games threatens to terminate his consistently happy, love-filled relationship

---

[14] Tom Giratikanon, Josh Katz, David Leonhardt and Kevin Quealy. "Up Close on Baseball's Borders." *The New York Times*, The New York Times, 23 Apr. 2014, www.nytimes.com/interactive/2014/04/23/upshot/24-upshot-baseball.html. Accessed 28 Sept. 2017.
[15] Markovits, Andrei. Sport Politics and Society. University of Michigan, Ann Arbor Michigan. September,19 2017. Course Lecture.

with Lindsey, he chooses the Red Sox (until Lindsey runs across Fenway's field and allows him to love both her and the Red Sox). Team loyalty is an affectively based, emotional attachment that depicts the pre-modernity of baseball.

The pre-modern aspects of baseball cause the modern components to be superfluous in terms of spectator attendance and fan-base size. The primary reason devoted fans attend games is not for the final tally of points on the scoreboard, but for everything else that accompanies going to a baseball game. There is an aspect of familial comradery, a religious experience, a commitment to a team despite consistent disappointment, and a shared understanding for team passion. Media such as *Fever Pitch* continue to depict this side of baseball, the pre-modern elements, because movies can embody the romanticized version of our everyday actions and illustrate the truest feelings of our psyches; the pre-modern reasons are why fans love baseball. The modern aspects of the sport are not what draws devoted fans to attend games, are not why it is America's favorite pastime, rather the pre-modern elements are what continue to draw passionate fans to this sport.

# Polarization and Lobbying Influence of the Dodd-Frank Act

by Kyra Lyngklip

*From PolSci 381: Political Research Design*

Nominated by Eitan Paul (GSI), Nancy Burns (Faculty)

Kyra's research design is clear, comprehensive, and original. The quality of her synthesis and organization of existing academic literature on her topic and identification of gaps in this literature approximates graduate-level writing and thinking. Kyra's research design also features a rigorous discussion of data collection, measurement, and analysis, which provides a high degree of confidence that her research design could be implemented as a sophisticated honors thesis project.

*Eitan Paul*

# THE DODD-FRANK ACT: Polarization and Lobbying Influence

## Introduction

The Consumer Financial Protection Bureau has drawn significant bipartisan political support outside of Congress: 78% of all Americans support stronger rules against Wall Street (a cornerstone of the Dodd-Frank Act) – this includes 85% of Democratic voters, 81% of Independent voters and 67% of Republican voters (O'Brien). Despite strong bipartisan support, passing the Dodd-Frank Act was a contentious political battle. Today, strong divisions over Dodd-Frank remain in Congress, with Republicans continuing efforts to deconstruct the Act and Democrats fighting to preserve it. Since Dodd-Franks' passage in 2010, Republicans in the House of Representatives have passed the CHOICE Act, which rolls back key parts of Dodd-Frank, with only 54% voting in favor (Civic Impulse, LLC). Other aspects of the Dodd-Frank Act have seen more severe polarization followed by reversals in policy. In October of 2017, the Senate voted to repeal the CFPB's arbitration rule by a single tie-breaker vote. Again, very different levels of polarization in Congress and in the electorate can be observed: despite almost perfect gridlock in Congress over the arbitration rule, a recent phone survey by a GOP polling company found that 64% of Republicans, 67% of independents and 74% of Democrats *support* the arbitration rule (Lane).

What accounts for this discrepancy? Why is the Dodd-Frank Act a polarizing issue in Congress but not among average citizens? One possible cause of this discrepancy is the influence of interest groups: members of Congress are lobbied by interest groups but average citizens are not. The provisions of Dodd-Frank are ripe for interest group mobilization because it affects two highly influential interests: consumer interests and financial interests. The consumer interest aspect of Dodd-Frank most likely explains bipartisan support in the electorate: Democratic and Republican citizens are united in the fact that they are all consumers. In the Dodd-Frank landscape, public interest groups such as Americans for Financial Reform have coalesced to lobby on behalf of diffuse interests of consumer protection. On the other side, many private interest groups representing the financial industry have lobbied avidly against Dodd-Frank in order to secure looser regulations over the financial industry. For example, the meeting in which the CFPB's arbitration rule was officially reversed was attended by several private interest lobbying groups: Consumer Bankers Association, Independent Community Bankers of America, National Association of Federally-Insured Credit Unions (Lane).

Since 1970, strictness of financial regulation has been on a steady decline. Under the Obama administration, financial regulation spiked higher than it had in 40 years, despite the presence of different political majorities in Congress over this period. Dodd-Frank represented the culmination of this spike in 2010. As the political landscape has shifted since 2010, the financial interest lobbying groups have successfully obtained reversals in key measures of Dodd-Frank that public opinion does not support. Further, Congressional support has become increasingly divided, yet definitively leaning towards favorable outcomes for these private financial interests. The turn toward public interest embodied in Dodd-Frank is surrounded on both sides by political trends favoring private interests and relatively laxer financial regulations. Thus, Dodd-Frank is an interesting policy case because it has undergone recent rollbacks its of key features even though the majority of the electorate supports it. Similar cases of majority bipartisan electorate support and a polarized Congress on the same issue exist, such as gun control policy. However, many of these cases, including the gun control case, have not seen as significant spikes in legislation representing the public, bipartisan interest as Dodd-Frank (Kurtzleben). In this regard, I argue that Dodd-Frank is markedly different from historical precedent and that public interest lobbying influence was unusually high which led to larger amounts of polarization and a less predictable eventual outcome for the Dodd-Frank Act.

This research proposal attempts to understand this unusual case by examining the cracks through which different types of lobbying groups were able to leverage their influence. While many scholars have also studied lobbying influence, many have struggled to capture a variety of factors in their measures such as a measure of influence that adjusts over time and political climate or that accounts for coalescing lobbying groups. Additionally, while some scholars have observed simple positive correlations between lobbying influence and polarization in Congress, few have empirically established their relationship from a causal standpoint (and none to date have done this on the specific case of Dodd-Frank). These findings will have implications on the larger question of how long the Dodd-Frank Act will last politically, and whether lobbying influence will play any part in that. It will also raise implications on the conditions in which private interests are able to successfully lobby against the common good/public interest.

## Literature Review

One key aspect missing in the current scholarly debate on Dodd-Frank is the degree to which private and public lobbying influence affect polarization in Congress. Some scholars have found that polarization, or political climate in general, can make or break the influence that interest groups hold over Congress. Capture theorists hold that influence of industry interest groups have strong sway over Congress member's decisions to legislate over those industries. Opponents of capture theory hold that public interest groups can have a strong sway over Congress member's decisions to legislate for the common good. However, no literature to date measures the politicizing effects of these countervailing forces. To build an understanding of these countervailing lobbying forces' effect on polarization of Congress, I will outline the components of lobbying influence, capture theory, and the weaknesses and strengths of private and public interest groups. Then, I will make some conclusions about how the existing literature affects my research method which measures lobbying influence's effect on the polarization in Congress.

# Components of Interest Group Influence: Alliances, Political Climate in Congress, and the Unheavenly Chorus

Bykerk and Maney find a factor of interest groups influence that many other scholars fail to account for – the political environment in Congress. They found that public interest groups representing consumer protection still received attention and were able to participate in consumer protection hearings even in more polarized and conservative political environments. However, public interest groups still saw waning relative influence in comparison to private lobbying powers. On the other hand, Kastner's research focuses on 2008, a much more liberal and "welcoming" environment to consumer interests. I include Kastner's work because it focuses on the opposite political climate of Bykerk and Maney's focus. By comparing the two literatures, I am able to see if the relationship between political climate and public interest lobby's ability to enlist elite partnerships remains constant across different political dominances in Congress. Both studies found that each respective lobbying group's influence and success depended on their ability to obtain allies. And in turn, each lobbying group's ability to obtain allies depended on the political climate –Republican or Democrat dominated (Woolley and Ziegler). Bykerk and Maney found that as political environments grew either more polarized or more conservative, public interest groups were less welcome to meet with individual Congress members and had more difficulty enlisting them as champions of their causes. Culpepper and Raphael argue that business interest's ability to enlist allies has allowed them to maintain their historical dominance in regulatory legislation because they have informal channels to access the political elite that other actors do not.

Schlozman, along with many other scholars, suggests that one way that private interests have been able to reach informal channels of access is through resources. Scholzman refers to this common phenomenon as "the unheavenly chorus that sings with a monied accent." That is, even though public interest groups may have broad support or other factors that would improve their salience may be present (such as an advantageous political environment), private interests are still able to make their voices heard better because they inevitably have more resources (money) to influence and buy access to Congress members. Kastner, Bykerk, and Maney all point to this same fact that consumer interest groups have weak resources compared to the financial lobby.

Scholzman's work embodies the commonly held view among scholarly discussion of lobbying influence that the more money and resources a lobbying group has, the more likely it is to be influential. Additionally, Schlozman's idea of the "heavenly chorus" is especially observable in more polarized or conservative political environments because under these conditions the private lobby has access to a key outlet to "sing" that the consumer lobby does not: buying access to individual Congress members.

## The Smaller Role of Public Interests and Capture Theory

Carpenter agrees that political climate can be a key determinant of whether interest groups see policy outcomes that align with their goals. However, Carpenter asserts that polarization and gridlock is much more an institutional development where minority leaders jockey for political support simply by doing the opposite of the majority in hopes that "if [voters] are dissatisfied, [they will] vote against the majority or incumbent." So, unlike Kastner, Mahoney and Bykerk, Carpenter largely dismisses the influence of interest groups on polarization and focuses more on the strategies politicians use to keep their seat in Congress. Carpenter's work exemplifies mainstream scholarly arguments for capture theory while also staying specific to Dodd-Frank. Also, Carpenter presents the null hypothesis to my research question: that there is little influence of lobbying activity (mostly public interest lobbying activity) on Congressional behavior. Instead, Carpenter argues that the outcome of a policy is more reliant on inside institutional factors.

Most scholars agree that public interest groups have the deck stacked against them when it comes to lobbying for regulation on an industry. Scholars, such as Carpenter, disregard the public interest lobby's influence on the legislative reform of Dodd-Frank and focus on the financial lobby's ability to stave off unwelcome change. This school of thought is referred to by scholars like Carpenter (along with Wilson, Stigler, and Olson) as capture theory. Capture theory holds that industry specific private interests have dominant influence on the regulations which govern their industry. Carpenter's work illustrates a common counter argument for regulatory capture over public interest. Carpenter recognizes that the support of public interest groups played a part in passing financial reform legislation. However, Carpenter focuses more closely on the shortcomings of public interest lobby and the ability of financial lobby to prevent stronger regulations from passing and even its ability to roll back aspects of Dodd-Frank.

## An Argument for Public Interest Influence: Rethinking Capture Theory

The literature of Trumbull, Ziegler and Woolley are valuable to the discussion of public interest influence because their arguments stand among the few that are Dodd-Frank specific (unlike Olson and other capture theorists). Their work also presents an explanation of the unique ability of consumer advocates to out-lobby big financial interests in the case of Dodd-Frank. Both literatures are unified in the fact that their research suggests a need for a reformed view of capture theory when considering public interest influence and Dodd-Frank. Where capture theory scholars point to the financial lobby's cohesiveness as a strength, Ziegler, Woolley, and Trumbull argue that public interest's diversity represents a unique strength that private interest groups cannot compete with. Trumbull's research contends with Mancur Olson, in addition to the argument of other capture theorist, and offers new explanations of the power of diffuse interests with respect to the legislation of Dodd-Frank. Olson argues that the larger the number of individuals in an interest group, the less likely it is to succeed. Olson reasons that lobbying is successful when concentrated interests of a few outweigh the many.

On the other hand, Trumbull concludes that because diffuse interests broadly advocate for the majority of individuals, they are able to draw strength and resources in their mobilization for policy reform based on moral legitimacy and the common good. Ziegler and Woolley argue that public interest lobbying is inherently diverse because, like Trumbull asserts, it represents the interests of the majority. Because of this diversity, apart from Trumbull's "moral legitimacy," private interests are at a disadvantage in the lobbying frontier. Ziegler and Woolley point to the example of Dodd-Frank where private interests could not contend "with the diffuse network of independent experts, advocacy organizations, former regulators, and other actors who also supplied a range of intellectual resources to pro-reform regulators." While Ziegler and Woolley do acknowledge that the financial lobby still maintains dominant influence over public interests, they find that capture theory does not accurately reflect the events in the legislation of Dodd-Frank since public interest lobbyists were able to obtain success in their lobbying efforts.

## Lobbying Influence: Troubling Measurements

One key aspect that frames the debate of lobbying influence is whether or not the scholars viewed the lobbying efforts (for both public and private interests) on the Dodd-Frank issue as a success or a failure. Kastner, Maney and Bykerk, and Ziegler and Woolley viewed Dodd-Frank as a success where public interests triumphed over the regulatory capture, despite a low budget. On the other hand, Carpenter argues that private interests were able to hinder, weaken, or roll back key regulations despite a political climate that was hostile to private interests. In this regard, it is important to create an objective measure of success so as not to either overestimate or underestimate influence of public and private interests in Congressional voting behavior. On a similar note, lobbying influence does not cease to exist after a piece of legislation is passed. Dodd-Frank has been modified many times after its passage in 2010. These modifications have been at least in part due to sustained efforts of lobbyists on both sides. Thus, a lobbyist's success changes as the legislation changes over time. Building in a dynamic measure of success will more accurately reflect on lobbying influence than focusing solely on the pre-passage lobbying efforts of Dodd-Frank. This can be done through the inclusion of related policy outcomes/reversion points after the passage of Dodd-Frank which is reflected in the data collection.

Another area of concern for measurement is the informal channels through which lobbyists secure elite allies. This is a more difficult measurement because most of the methods that measure lobbying influence focus solely on role call voting, lobbyist appearances in hearings, speech patterns, or the numbers of successes and failures of lobbyists on policy outcomes. Data on informal channels such as private discussions or meetings with Congress members may be particularly difficult to access because the information is inherently private. A way to tackle this in the research method might be to ask lobbying groups to list any contact with legislators outside of hearings or formal meetings in a survey. Additionally, the survey could also ask lobbying groups to list allies in Congress that aligned with their cause.

Just because a lobbying group possesses all the components that scholars say are indicative to influence (such as elite alliances, an advantageous political climate, immense resources, and regulatory capture) does not mean that the lobbying group will actually be influential. This was true in the case of Dodd-Frank where private interest groups in Washington failed to achieve their lobbying goals (which had many of the components of influence), and consumer advocates saw a decrease in regulatory capture as a result of their lobbying efforts. Thus, measurements of lobbying influence must distinguish expected influence, which would favor big financial lobby, from true, observable influence, which would favor consumer advocates. This distinction is crucial in building a research model that correctly measures the sway of each opposing lobby over the political climate in Congress.

## Looking Past Lobbying Influence: Polarization Expectations

Many scholars think of polarization on a certain policy issue in terms of ideological dimensionality. Jochim and Jones and Poole and Rosenthal have measured the effects of political issue's dimensionality on Congress members' voting behavior in respects to political ideology. Scholars studying this issue have often operationalized dimensionality by how easy a certain policy issue may be fit into a political ideology. In this respect, understanding the political dimensionality of sub-issues of Dodd-Frank will allow us to predict the degree of polarization in Congress based on contending lobbying forces on that issue. We will also be able to test a key alternative hypothesis: that certain members simply vote for or against a unidimensional issue because they can easily fit their position on that issue according to their ideal point/ideology (Jochim and Jones; Poole and Rosenthal). This hypothesis discounts the fact that lobbying influence can decide how a member might vote. Because we can measure how closely Congress members maintain their ideological integrity on an issue-by-issue basis, we can see how this varies by policy dimensionality – primarily financial legislation (a unidimensional policy issue) and consumer protection legislation (a multidimensional policy issue). Accounting for political dimensions of the legislation of interest is especially important because supporters of consumer protection initiatives embodied in Dodd-Frank have some very notable outliers among the Republican Party which would need to be taken into special consideration with reliable variability measurements of polarization.

# Research Design

## Variables and Hypotheses Overview

I hypothesize that the lobbying landscape of Dodd-Frank saw unusually high levels of public interest influence because, in line with public interest scholars, not only did the public interest lobby have a favorable political climate, its ability to coordinate a diverse web of resources allowed access to other factors of influence such as allies. Additionally, I hypothesize that high levels of polarization in Congress on the issue of the Dodd-Frank Act is caused by lobbying group influence. This is because the opposing lobbying groups are polarized in their policy aims. So if either (and most likely both) public and private interest lobbying groups are meaningfully influential on the voting behavior of Congress, it will have a polarizing effect on Congress as a whole. More specifically, public interest lobbying groups will have a greater polarizing effect on more multidimensional facets of Dodd-Frank. Private interest lobbying groups will have a greater polarizing effect on unidimensional facets of Dodd-Frank since they tend to seek out unidimensional policy aims (looser financial regulation). Public interest lobbying groups will have a greater polarizing effect on multidimensional facets of Dodd-Frank since they tend to seek out multidimensional policy aims (expansion of consumer protection).

The central independent variable is lobbying group influence which will vary by public interest lobbying groups representing diffuse interests and private interest lobbying groups representing concentrated interests. My dependent variable is the polarization of Congress on the issue of Dodd-Frank Act as seen through voting patterns, speeches, and proposed countervailing legislation.

Many scholars have pointed to the alternative hypothesis that rather than lobbying influence leading to increased polarization in Congress, increased polarization or certain political conditions open a window for some interest groups to spread their influence over policy outcomes (see Kastner's "policy window"). This alternative hypothesis flips the hypothesized independent and dependent variables. It asserts that lobbying influence depends on the political conditions in Congress. Correlation does not equal causation. To control for such a causal confusion, measures of influence will be stratified by a variety of confounding variables such as passage of time, political climate, unity votes maintaining ideological integrity, and success. This stratification influence will also allow us to test Carpenter's alternative hypothesis: that polarization is in fact not a product of lobbying influence but ideological integrity of Congress members or other institutional dynamics.

## Independent Variable: Lobbying Influence

I will derive a score of influence based on how the literature has defined it. The main components of an influence score will consist of resources (such as the presence of a full time lobbyist or high levels of campaign contribution), ability to obtain elite alliances, and political climate in Congress (in reference to Kastner's Policy Window theory). I will combine these measurements with Bernhagen et al.'s approach to measure my independent variable. This approach is unique from most other models on the subject in that it measures the influence of interest groups spatially.

I will use Berhagen's spatial model to compare interest groups' resources and strategies (defined as influence) with the preferences of interest groups and the extent of their satisfaction with the policy outcome (defined as success). Success of interest groups is divided into an objective and subjective score, measuring each score with qualitative and quantitative data. The objective success score encompasses quantitative (primarily frequency of hearing appearances) and qualitative data to gauge interest group success on a scale ranging from "not at all" to "fully." The subjective approach will use primarily qualitative data from surveys sent to policymakers and interest groups to code dichotomously whether interest groups perceived the policy outcomes reached some, none, or all of their policy preferences on an ordinal scale. I will also base my data collection methods off of the models in Bernhagen et al. To obtain the data to measure lobbying influence, I will use policy positions of lobbying groups on consumer and financial policy issues from the time of 1970 up until 2017, while also collecting data on frequency of hearing attendance and administering surveys to those same groups to fill in their scores of influence as previously defined.

Bernhagen et al. aggregated success scores by group type with respect to four policy domains which then measured success of interest group influence by distance from their policy outcome preferences. Similarly, I will do this but with only two policy domains: consumer protection and financial regulation. By using this measure, I will be weighing the distance between the interest group's ideal point against the overall policy outcome to measure influence. I will then be able to see which type of interest groups have more influence for a unidimensional policy domain (financial regulation) and for a multidimensional policy domain. Successful lobbying groups under each domain will bring policy outcomes closer to their preferences, and unsuccessful policy actors will bring policy outcomes farther away from their preferences. -measures – qualitative and quantitative.

One major weakness in this method appears when it comes to measuring ideal points of interest groups as opposed to Poole and Rosenthal's ideal points of Congress member's: Bernhagen et al.'s methods do not account for the policy outcome's reversion point (the final position in circumstances of a legislative agreement *over time*). This is particularly problematic for my research because since 2010, there have been several significant reversions in the Dodd-Frank Act. To account for this weakness, I will use a *third* spatial measure from Bernhagen et al.'s methods to examine relative improvement compared to the reversion point by the distance that an actor has to the final outcome called the improvement-to-reversion point. Using this third spatial measure, Bernhagen et al. conducted a two-step test in which they first held the policy outcome constant and varied the reversion point, and, second, varied the policy outcome and held the reversion point constant. They found these measures to be independent (the outcome of one did not affect the outcome of the other) and thus found that their objective and subjective spatial measures of public interest group success to be accurate and did not vary with the potentially confounding variable of the reversion point.

The question of interest is whether, accounting for these reversion points, public interest groups on the issue of Dodd-Frank will be successful over time. I will know if public interest groups are successful over time, if the data that continues from 2010-2017 shows that they do fall closer to their ideal points on the spatial model. Most importantly, the interest groups with the highest success will be closest to their ideal points when reversion point measures we subtract reversion points (Bernhagen et al.; Poole and Rosenthal).

Scholars have praised this method because existing literature has found different conclusions about the success of interest groups depending on whether the study uses objective or subjective measures. Since this method accounts for both, and reversion points (which is highly relevant to Dodd-Frank which is could potentially has seen significant reversions) it seems to be the most holistic and applicable approach for measuring influence of interest groups. The breadth of data used in this model also allows the testing of various hypothesis and stratifies influence so that it will mostly likely vary for every single interest group whose data the model uses. Also, unlike other studies on the matter, it pays special attention to interest group characteristics and tactics through surveys that cannot be observed in traditional quantitative data sets which will allow me to address my measurement concerns of informal meetings and alliances, among other nuanced characteristics of influence. Thus, this method allows for more representative data and more valid measures of influence rather than simply measuring the idea of success (another measurement concern) as a measure of influence.

## Dependent Variable: Polarization in Congress

After using Bernhagen et al.'s spatial model to measure influence, we will be able to see the degree of polarization each lobbying group inflicts over a policy outcome. This next set of measurements over polarization in Congress will "zoom in" to see the degree of political division/polarization within these outcomes. To measure polarization in Congress, I will base my model off of Jochim and Jones' model. Jochim and Jones' model nuances the Poole and Rosenthal NOMINATE model of polarization by measuring polarization across policy dimensionality. Jochim and Jones measure the effects of political issue's dimensionality on Congress members' voting behavior in respects to political ideology by scaling roll call votes on hot-button issues from 1947 to 2004. Similarly, my data for measuring polarization will be comprised of roll call votes on consumer protection and financial regulation from the period of 1970 to 2017.

This is especially important because from this data set, I will be able to compare patterns of polarization in the "golden age" of financial regulation (a 30-year period starting in the 1970s noted for its continued relaxation of financial regulations), to the period of 2008-2012 during which the trends of the "golden age" reversed, and from 2012 on where policy outcomes gradually revert back to the "golden age" trend. The selection of this data set can also be used to test Kastner's Policy Window alternative hypothesis because congressional voting patterns reflect the degree of polarization in Congress across periods of republican and democrat dominated Congresses.

We can then compare these different periods with the amount of successes public and private interest groups see within each period to find if political climate causes the degree of influence of certain interest groups. In this way, the data will allow us to understand any unusual spike in financial regulation and consumer protection measures in reference to the political climate and amount of political division in which it occurred.

Jochim and Jones's method establishes the causation behind the correlations between Congressional ideological integrity and unidimensional policy areas. To do this, Jochim and Jones look at polarization on an issue-by-issue basis. A key step in finding why the polarization occurs for Jochim and Jones was to measure dimensionality with extremely rigorous coding procedures for the dimensionality of a policy issue (more rigorous than the existing models by Poole and Rosenthal). To reduce subjectivity in coding dimensionality of policy issues up for vote in Congress, Jochim and Jones used Catell's "elbow test" which charts eigenvalues against each dimension (if there is a sharp change that resembles an elbow, another dimension must be added to the coding of the policy issue). Then, to double check if unidimensional policy issues have been coded correctly, Jochim and Jones calculated the proportion of variance of the first eigenvalue. If the proportion is low, then the policy issue is coded as unidimensional. Then, to evaluate party cohesion of the coded policy issue, Jochim and Jones calculated the corresponding proportion of party unity votes.

The proportions of party cohesion are then aggregated and compared to dimensionality to see the where polarization is present in Congressional voting. I will also apply these coding procedures to my own data of roll call votes on consumer protection and financial regulation from the period of 1970 to 2017.

The measurements should show that if policy issues represent unidimensional issues, then the researcher will find variability across policy issues, an evolution over time, and increased party cohesion. Jochim and Jones found that this was in fact true from their own data: on unidimensional policy issues such as economy, there was strong increases in party cohesion and greater polarization. On multi-dimensional issues such as civil rights, there was weaker party cohesion and smaller polarization. Similarly, in our measurements, we expect to see greater polarization on financial regulations and lesser polarization on the multidimensional issue of consumer protection if our hypothesis is true. By segregating policy issues by dimension and comparting levels of polarization, we will be able to test the alternative hypothesis that Congress members polarize Congress by simply voting according to their ideal point. If this is true, we should not see comparable levels of polarization for each type of policy issue. However, if we observe equal or higher levels of polarization on consumer protection policy issues in the case of Dodd-Frank, what we observe will be markedly different from historical trends and capture theory in favor or our hypothesis.

## Data Analysis

In our measurements of polarization and lobbying influence, we have hopefully accounted for enough confounding variables in our measures of influence and polarization to establish some causal inferences about our primary and alternative hypotheses. We can compare the degree of polarization across distinct categories: public vs. private interest groups and unidimensional versus multi-dimensional policy issues and political climate (Republican dominated or Democrat dominated Congress).

After we have found our measurements of polarization and lobbying influence, we can compare two measures to make some conclusions about our hypotheses using linear regression. Overall, we will be using our measures of lobbying influence per group to see the amount of political division it causes in Congress. First and foremost, we will know whether our hypothesis is correct if we see public interest groups exhibit higher volumes of lobbying success (based on spatial score units) *and* polarization (found with the dependent variable). On our linear regression for unidimensional issues we will see a positive correlation between polarization and lobbying influence for private interests. On our linear regression for multidimensional issues we will see a positive correlation between polarization and lobbying influence for public interests. We can also see how polarization relates to political issue dimensionality since we used a coding scheme that expresses dimensionality quantitatively. With this information, we can test the alternative hypothesis that members vote to maintain party cohesion (that they vote only according to their ideology). If this is true we should see a negative correlation: as political dimensionality on an issue increases, polarization decreases. If our hypothesis is correct, that public and private lobbying groups both have meaningful influence, we should see corresponding Congressional voting behavior that results in equal levels of polarization.

We will also compare this relationship to differences in political climate to see if these findings remain stable across political climate. To see this result would mean that for each category, we will find that lobbying behavior influences Congressional behavior to the point of polarization. We will need to compare each of these measures to the measures found for Dodd-Frank to see if private and public interest groups are seeing similar or anomalous influences on polarization. We might see the opposite result if we are wrong, however, this is highly unlikely as public interest groups tend to lobby for multidimensional policy outcomes and private interests tend to lobby for more unidimensional outcomes (Bernhagen et al.). The more likely outcome that would suggest we are wrong would be that the relationships between influence and polarization do not remain stable across different political climates. This outcome would favor the policy window argument.

# Conclusion

The first and most important next step will be to collect data. Since my research design uses mixed methods with a variety of confounding variables over a wide period of time, I will be using mixed sources of data. I am also hoping to use some data from the following scholars' work: Bykerk and Maney, Kastner, Jochim and Jones, and Poole and Rosenthal. Together, these data sets will cover the majority of my research interests. However, I will most likely need to do the remainder of the data collection myself, focusing on the period of 2010 to 2017 to account for reversion points in policies relevant to my research design. The most critical data collection will be the surveys of lobbying groups for my measure of lobbying influence. Ideally, I would like to travel to D.C. and perform interviews instead of sending out a survey. With interviews, I would have a greater awareness of what amount of non-response bias I can expect (rather than just sending out a survey to lobbying groups hoping that I receive back a response).

I would also like to spend some more time dealing with the problem of success and influence. I have recently become aware that many public interest groups coalesced while lobbying for the Dodd-Frank Act (Pagliari). Separating out success and influence measurements for coalescing groups may become problematic in that some smaller, less influential groups that coalesced with larger groups may be falsely measured as highly influential by mere association and vice versa for larger groups. With more time, I will incorporate a (hopefully) effective measure to account for the issue of coalescing lobbying groups.

# Bibliography

"H.R. 10: Financial CHOICE Act of 2017." 2017. October 1. GovTrak.

Bernhagen, Patrick, Andreas Dür, and David Marshall. 2014. "Measuring Lobbying Success Spatially." *Interest Groups & Advocacy* 3 (2):202.

Bykerk, Loree, and Ardith Maney. 2010. "Consumer Protection Policy Issues on the Congressional Agenda." *Political Science Quarterly* 125 (4):639-55.

Carpenter, Daniel. 2010. "Institutional Strangulation: Bureaucratic Politics and Financial Reform in the Obama Administration." *Perspectives on Politics* 8 (3):825-46.

Culpepper, Pepper D., and Raphael Reinke. 2014. "Structural Power and Bank Bailouts in the United Kingdom and the United States." *Politics & Society* 42 (4) (12/01; 2017/12):427-54.

Jochim, Ashley E., and Bryan D. Jones. 2013. "Issue Politics in a Polarized Congress." *Political Research Quarterly* 66 (2):352-69.

Kastner, Lisa. 2014. "'Much Ado about Nothing?' Transnational Civil Society, Consumer Protection and Financial Regulatory Reform." *Review of International Political Economy* 21 (6):1313.

———. 2017. "Tracing Policy Influence of Diffuse Interests: The Post-Crisis Consumer Finance Protection Politics in the US." *Journal of Civil Society* 13 (2) (04/03):130-48.

Kay Lehman Schlozman, Sidney Verba, and Henry E. Brady. 2012. *The Unheavenly Chorus*. US: Princeton University Press.

Kurtzleben, Danielle. 2017. "**Poll: Majorities Of Both Parties Favor Increased Gun Restrictions.**" December 10. https://www.npr. org/2017/10/13/557433452/poll-majorities-of-both-parties-favor-increased-gun-restrictions.

Lane, Sylvan. 2017. "Trump repeals consumer arbitration rule, wins banker praise." November 3.

Mahoney, Christine. 2007. "Lobbying Success in the United States and the European Union." *Journal of Public Policy* 27 (1):35.

Olson, Mancur. 1971; [1971, c1965]. *The Logic of Collective Action; Public Goods and the Theory of Groups*. New York: Schocken Books.

Pagliari, Stefano, and Kevin L. Young. 2014. "Leveraged Interests: Financial Industry Power and the Role of Private Sector Coalitions." *Review of International Political Economy* 21 (3) (05/04):575-610.

Poole, Keith T., and Howard Rosenthal. 1997. *Congress: A Political-Economic History of Roll Call Voting*. New York: Oxford University Press.

Trumbull, Gunnar. 2012. *Strength in Numbers: The Political Power of Weak Interests*. Cambridge, Mass.: Harvard University Press.

Ziegler, J. N., and John T. Woolley. 2016. "After Dodd-Frank." *Politics & Society* 44 (2):249.

# Winning Essays
## Granader Prize for Excellence in Upper-Level Writing (humanities)

## Human Agency and Control in the Shadow of Enlightenment

by Mateusz Borowiecki

*From German 401: European Intellectual and Cultural History from Revolution to World War*

Nominated by Scott Spector

This is a wonderfully animated paper with an argument that drives it forward. What we love about this argument is its capacity to sustain paradox and contradiction, while still somehow remaining consistent and committed to its argumentation. It is a creative if polemical argument. The skills displayed here at weaving together the threads running through an array of very different thinkers are impressive.

*Scott Spector*

# Human Agency and Control in the Shadow of Enlightenment

When asked "What is Enlightenment?", Immanuel Kant famously replied "Enlightenment is man's release from his self-incurred tutelage" (Kant, 1784). From its very inception, Enlightenment was synonymous with a human liberation of sorts. On the material end, Enlightenment meant the growth of science, and the comprehension and control of natural forces for the benefit of mankind. But additionally, it meant man trusting in his own reason rather than acquiescing to the judgment of "guardians" to comprehend the world for him: "if I have a book to serve as my understanding, a pastor to serve as my conscience, a physician to determine my diet for me, and so on, I need not exert myself at all. I need not think". Thus Enlightenment meant using reason to reclaim agency from both the natural world and the social order and granting it to the individual. "Nothing is required for this enlightenment", writes Kant, "except freedom".

And yet, the principles of the Enlightenment were ultimately antithetical to this sort of human liberation. The Enlightenment's scientists, in exploring the natural world, discovered that even the most marvelous phenomena, like the movements of the heavenly bodies, could be explained and predicted with immaculate precision through the unmasking of universal, fundamental laws, like gravity. These fundamental laws seemed capable of explaining the entire universe: gravity and the laws of motion and energy in physics, the patterns of interaction and reaction in chemistry, and later, the processes of evolution through the mechanism of natural selection in biology. So it should come as no surprise that this same framework was soon applied to human society as well, as a multitude of thinkers across the late 18th and 19th century applied the reasoning spirit of the Enlightenment to reveal the fundamental laws of human operation. Yet this search for human nature, far from emancipating man, characterized him as merely a slave to some immutable, intrinsic characteristic, and furthermore justified the construction of social systems that controlled man all the more rather than liberating him. The "rationalization" of human action, far from liberating humankind, only drove humanity into an "iron cage" of controlling institutions, as was only realized by Max Weber and other 20th century critics facing the horrors of "scientific" ideologies, the end result of the Enlightenment mindset.

Just as chemists and physicists could extract some equation to explain the behavior of the inorganic substances they studied, so too did the earliest social thinkers of this period seek some simple mathematical solution to the problem of human action. The earliest attempt at reducing human society down to some general mathematical rule can be seen in Thomas Malthus' infamous essay on population growth. His argument can be summarized in the following lines:

*Population, when unchecked, increases in a geometrical ratio. Subsistence increases only in an arithmetical ratio. A slight acquaintance with numbers will show the immensity of the first power in comparison to the second.* (Malthus, 1798)

The argument seems simple enough: by some fundamental law, food demand grows faster than food supply. But where does this assumption come from? Browsing the text up and down, one is unable to find any sort of empirical justification for the belief in the stated geometrical and arithmetical growth. Is it an argument from history? This is certainly not unheard of: even contemporary histories of, for example, medieval Europe (see e.g. Cantor, 1994) resort to a Malthusian argument to explain why in the long run, improvements in agricultural productivity did not result in an increase in the standard of living. However, few references to any empirical study of history can be found in Malthus' writing: instead, he refers to "fixed laws of our nature" to explain the pattern. I say no "empirical" study because Malthus does claim that "these two laws, ever since we have had any knowledge of mankind, appear to have been fixed", indicating a vague historical claim. However, how Malthus jumps from a stylized historical fact, that *generally* food production does not grow faster than population, and leaps to a *specific* mathematical formula is not made clear anywhere in the text.

If anything, Malthus seems to be adopting a facsimile of mathematical rigor to his social claims in order to legitimize his claims: you can't deny the numbers! It is, hence, an "absolute impossibility from the fixed laws of our nature, that the pressure of want can ever be completely removed from the lower classes of society".

Malthus is, of course, correct: if one accepts the numbers, one must also accept the implications of those numbers, which have the power of mathematical certainty behind them. A similar trend can be seen in the work of Jeremy Bentham, a highly influential British social thinker writing starting in the late 18th century. Taking a much more systematic approach to the issue compared to Malthus, Bentham wrote what is essentially a manual for understanding and categorizing human behavior, with the clear end goal of converting human action into a maximization function of sorts. "The general tendency of an act", he writes, "is more or less pernicious according to the total sum of its consequences" (Bentham, 1780). He also rejects any deontological impetus of action, stating that "goodness or badness can't properly be predicated of motives". This leaves just one principle upon which society should be design: the maximization of pleasure against pain—a simple mathematical exercise, should man learn how to measure these values accurately. Bentham does not shy away from this, stating "pleasures and the avoidance of pains, then, are the legislator's goals"; he later adds that "the business of government is to promote the happiness of society by punishing and rewarding".

That last section is especially important. For if all is reduced down to a faction that needs maximizing, then, well, *someone* needs to be doing that maximizing! A similar proposition is made explicit within Malthus's text: if one is to avoid the pain of the positive check, the lower classes, so bound to their innate nature, must be kept in line via preventive checks instead, rules regulating behavior imposed from above. Writing within two decades of Kant, two major Enlightenment social thinkers are already firm in their beliefs which seem antithetical to Kant's original proclamation of Enlightenment as liberation from tutelage, or from immaturity[1]. For Malthus, the great bulk of the population can never emerge from such immaturity themselves, bound as they are to laws of reproduction until utter starvation deprives them of their ability to have more children. Likewise for Bentham, there is little hope that individuals alone can maximize happiness: Bentham calls upon the government to instead administer punishment and reward upon empirical investigation of the matter[2]. Having allegedly discovered some base driving factors of the human condition and human behavior through the empirical machinations of Enlightenment reasoning, they now wish to place the bulk of humanity *back under tutelage* for their own good. These early empirical studies of the social, by seeking out *universal* rules of action for human beings, necessarily reduced humans into mere puppets of these external laws. Sapped of their ability to reason beyond these conditions, only able to act according to these rules, man would either live in misery or be compelled to submit himself to the tutelage of the state. Enlightenment only served to control man further, not liberate him.

The end result of such essentialist fever dreams must necessarily be a figure like John Galton, the British polymath who first coined the term "eugenics"— once science had advanced far enough to give concrete empirical grounding for a theory of eugenics, that is. Galton was, indeed, the ultimate biological essentialist: whereas a figure like Malthus had to rely on intuition and casual observation, Galton had comprehensive evolutionary theory backing him up; where Malthus had to limit himself to writing pamphlets, Galton set up laboratories to study, measure, observe and ultimately attempt to influence the biology of his subjects firsthand[3]. Of course, this rationalization of the biological theory was its ultimate

[1] The translation of this first sentence of Kant's text varies significantly. Some sources translate it as "emergence from nonage", others as liberation from "immaturity" or "tutelage". I have elected to use "tutelage" in this essay, as I believe it is a word both familiar to a contemporary audience and closest in meaning to the original German Unmündigkeit in this context.

[2] "The business of government is to promote the happiness of the society by punishing and rewarding" (Bentham, 1780); much of the text is dedicated to describing how legislators can best implement such rewards and punishments in order to best achieve their utilitarian goal.

[3] Thanks in part to Galton's advocacy, by the 1920s many notable universities around the world hosted eugenics departments, with 376 American universities offering courses in the subject (Selden, 2005).

downfall: once a specific scientific theory which makes substantive empirical predictions is formulated, it can be equally empirically refuted through scientific investigation. And so when the ideas of biological essentialism, now scientifically formulated as eugenics, were confronted with contradictory scientific evidence regarding their efficacy, they had no choice but to collapse. Not before doing extensive damage to the world around them first, of course: across the West, half-baked eugenicist theories had led to the sterilization or murder of millions.

By comparison, the idea of society crafted by Adam Smith, the other major early social thinker, seems positively utopian. His proto-Durkheimian vision of peaceful coexistence through mutual economic interdependence between specialized actors certainly seems to avoid the authoritarian spectre of other early Enlightenment social thinkers, and appears as a breath of fresh air among the wave of interventionist proposals of his era. This is not to say that Smith eschewed government entirely, of course. But by and large, on the face of it one could be forgiven for mistaking Smith's vision as one that is truly liberating, in the best spirit of Kant's Enlightenment. However, a closer examination proves that this is not the case.

First, the obvious must be stated: as was the case with Enlightenment thinkers after him, Smith too postulated some basic principle as defining human behavior and differentiating humanity at the fundamental level. In his case, it is "a certain propensity [...] to truck, barter, and exchange one thing for another" (Smith, 1776). He furthermore claims that this characteristic is "common to all men", and so while he admits that it is beyond his purview to determine whether the tendency is biological in nature, by claiming it as universal he implicitly claims that it is innate to all beings of our species. It is, of course, entirely uncontroversial that in any human social grouping, some form of transfer, frequently reciprocal, of goods or services occurs. At the minimum, one can think of nurturing one's young, a defining practice among all mammals, as necessitating some form of transfer and hence division of labor, even if it is something as simple as a parent foraging for food and transferring it to their young. To say that material things are transferred between humans living in social groups, and that this behavior is innate, is therefore trivial and irrelevant. What matters here is Smith's next assertion: "Give me that which I want, and you shall have this which you want, is the meaning of every such [exchange]; and it is in this manner that we obtain from one another the far greater part of those good offices which we stand in need of". By the transitive property, Smith here claims that markets and market exchange are intrinsic to humans, biologically or not.

There exists a broad and, at this point, ancient literature which questions the connection between markets and division of labor (see e.g. Polanyi (1944), Malinowski (1922)) which will not be addressed here, especially as it is not *directly* relevant to the central issue of this essay. Instead, one must ask: how does such a view affect the autonomy, the freedom from tutelage, of its subjects? Smith famously proclaimed that "it is not from the benevolence of the butcher, the brewer, or the baker, that we expect our dinner, but from their regard to their own interest". Smith here essentially implies that regardless of the personal feelings of the baker, brewer, or butcher, they must transact in order to survive in a society with highly specialized labor. Malthus actually notes a similar point, discussing how market prices effectively act as controls on individuals in spite of their internal desires: "there are some men, even in the highest rank, who are prevented from marrying by the idea of the expenses they must retrench," so that "these considerations undoubtedly prevent a great number in this rank of life from following the bent of their inclinations in an early attachment". Given Malthus' earlier claim that it takes something as strong as outright starvation to keep reproduction in check, these market forces must be powerful indeed!

Karl Marx reserves even stronger words on the tyranny of exchange in capitalist societies. "The division of labor implies the contradiction between the interest of the separate individual or the individual family and the communal intercourse of all individuals", he writes, echoing Smith's point that self-interest, not beneficence, motivate economic exchange (Marx, 1846). Indeed, when "activity is not voluntary, but naturally, divided, man's own deed becomes an alien power opposed to him, which enslaves him instead of being controlled by him". Furthermore, "as soon as the distribution of labor comes into being, each man has a particular, exclusive sphere of activity, which is forced upon him and from which he cannot escape". Marx describes the Smithian man as one that is enslaved, unable to escape, one whose control over his own life has been wrested from him. This is clearly evident: after all, *interdependence* includes **dependence!** More concretely, it should be evidently clear to every member of market society that prices exert some control over their decision-making—to put it in generous, Smithian terms, they internalize the costs associated with another producing the good for the one consuming it, causing them to, for example, consume less should the price rise not out of consideration for the welfare of some producing other, but out of their own material self-interest.

Whether what we can call the Smithian mode of social control, through price systems which internalize the costs incurred by others, as more or less tyrannical previous modes of social organization, for example the village community or the archaic guild system, is a separate question. In a sense it does not matter, since the point here is to illuminate systems of control for what they are rather than making ordinal claims about which control system is better or worse. The crucial part is that in this system, the individual loses control to the point where the bulk of his actions are determined by external forces alien to him. Indeed, the Smithian system of control is especially insidious in that there is no one controlling authority one can point to and accuse of tyranny. Whereas the Malthusian and Benthamite models imply or assume some central authority, usually the state, as the thing which places man under its tutelage, a Smithian market has no such "Big Bad". I may be dependent on others for my food supply, but there is no one farmer I can point to and shout "this guy is controlling me by charging me for food!" Indeed, there is such a complex network of food growers, suppliers, transporters and distributors that when I am faced with a final price at a grocery store, there remains no Big Bad to blame, but only the whole network of price-exchangers that ultimately formed and delivered the product—in a word, society. The market therefore appears as a sort of "force of nature" which I cannot control, and can only react to the prices it spits out at me. As a result, it is difficult to see the market as a form of social control, any more than one could accuse a hurricane of controlling one's actions. In such a market society, man ceases to be a free agent and becomes subject to pseudo-natural forces, just as Malthus and Bentham conceived of man as a slave to biological impulse and hedonistic pleasure, respectively. He is placed under the tutelage of the market. Just as Kant's pastor shouts "do not argue, pray!"; like his officer yells "do not argue, drill!", so too the Smithian man hears "do not argue, follow the price signal!"

The sociologist Alan G. Johnson once proposed the following scenario: a visiting Martian, casually observing a game of Monopoly, would be forgiven for concluding that man is incredibly selfish, spiteful, egoistic and unconcerned for the welfare of others (Johnson, 1997). Yet we know that this conclusion is just as unwarranted as concluding that humans are always cooperative, caring, considerate and pro-social from observing a game of, say, Pandemic[4]. That is to say, while it is evident that the rule systems individuals are placed in impact their behavior, if the system is complex and obscured well enough it can appear that behavior that is in reality emergent from the system is actually the result of innate characteristics. Psychologists will recognize this phenomenon as the fundamental attribution error[5], one of the best-attributed cognitive biases in behavioral research (Malle, 2006). This bias is what makes the Smithian worldview especially perfidious. The spirit of the Enlightenment may have been meant to illuminate a dark room: to make visible what was in shadow with the power of reason and empirical investigation. Yet in the social sphere, Enlightenment did not illuminate, but cast eerie shadows and generated strange colors. As Dr. Johnson's example makes clear, social systems form self-fulfilling prophecies: if we assume certain "natural" rules of operation, we construct systems which facilitate operation of

---

[4] A board game requiring the intimate cooperation of all players to achieve victory, commonly played by the author and fairly popular among kids these days more generally.

[5] From Malle (2006): "observers tend to attribute behavior to stable dispositions of the actor". Experiments have found that even when the cause of an outcome is clearly external, such as the completely random outcome of a coin flip, observers often ascribe blame to the individual, not the circumstances.

those rules, and actors within them will be forced to conform, making those rules seem all the more natural. And attribution error only reinforces this cycle.

The cruder essentialist theories were eventually dispelled by nature of their naturalistic tendencies: as Malthus evolved into Galton, the theory became more and empirical and hence disprovable through empirical methods where it contradicted biological truth. But theories of social systems not *explicitly* reliant on biological presuppositions prove themselves through ever-greater feedback loops. The Enlightenment may have had a penchant for agency-stripping social theories, but many of these disintegrated under empirical strain, something compounded by the failure and horror of "scientific" ideologies throughout the 20th century. It is no coincidence that of the thinkers discussed in this paper, only one—Adam Smith—remains popular. Malthus seems irrelevant; Galton's eugenics are popularly reviled; Bentham is recognized as essentially totalitarian; yet Smithian control marches on, if anything expanding its control over humanity since the dawn of the neoliberal era. Unlike the other, clearly essentialist theories discussed in this essay, it is unbearably difficult to perceive Smithian social control as, well, social control, because of the perception of agency through market choice on one hand, and the anthropomorphization of market forces as an "invisible hand": an external force with its own impenetrable will and whims that humanity is only ever subject to. The totalitarian social spirit of the Enlightenment still haunts the West today, even as the most obvious perpetrators have been nearly universally rejected.

Enlightenment reason attempted to decompose human behavior in a scientific manner into some fundamental principles, into merely the result of external or "dead" base forces, leaving nothing for an individual will or any sense of true agency. As a result, Enlightenment perspectives on humanity could only ever propose systems of social control, not social liberation, just as discovering the laws of chemistry and physics naturally led to man seizing control of the physical environment around him[6]. The most essentialist of these attempts were long thrown out; however, the most insidious one remains, even strengthens, into the present day. I will not go into detail regarding contemporary social development, but suffice it to say that there is compelling evidence that *perception* of agency, or a belief in an internal locus of control, has severely declined in the last forty years[7], as market forces have become a resurgent force in our daily lives[8]. It seems that evermore and against Kant's Enlightenment spirit, rationalization in the form of Smithian social control has placed humanity under the tutelage social forces so ubiquitous they seem nearly biological. "Do not argue, obey!"

---

[6] It is only recently that the Western mentality has been forced back into a "reactionary" posture regarding the natural world, largely due to the effects of climate change. Those following the popular literature will note, for example, how the rhetoric surrounding global warming has changed from stopping climate change, an agential position, to coping with climate change, a reactive stance.

[7] See for example, the research conducted by the Monitoring the Future project at the University of Michigan's Institute for Social Research. Their longitudinal survey of social attitudes has found that since the 70s, 20-30% more American high school seniors reply to survey questions in ways which indicate a belief in an "external nexus of control", or a belief that their life is controlled by external forces. For a more detailed exploration of these results, see Harris (2017).

[8] For a review of some of the literature on this topic, see Birch & Siemiatycki (2016).

Bibliography

Bentham, J. (1780). *An Introduction to the Principles of Morals and Legislation.*

Birch, K., & Siemiatycki, M. (2016). Neolibearlism and the geographies of marketization: The entangling of state and markets. *Human Geography.*

Cantor, N. F. (1994). *The Civilization of the Middle Ages.* Harper Collins.

Harris, M. (2017). *Kids These Days: Human capital and the making of millennials.* New York: Public Agenda.

Johnson, A. G. (1997). *The forest and the trees: sociology as life, practice, and promise.* Philadelphia: Temple University Press.

Kant, I. (1784). What is Enlightenment? In I. Kant, *Berlinische Monatsschrift Book.*

Malinowski, B. (1922). *Argonauts of the Western Pacific.*

Malle, B. F. (2006). The actor-observer asymmetry in attribution: A (surprising) meta-analysis. *Psychologial Bulletin*, 895-919.

Malthus, T. (1798). *An Essay on the Principle of Population.*

Marx, K. (1846). *The German Ideology.*

Polanyi, K. (1944). *The Great Transformation.*

Selden, S. (2005). Transforming better babies into fitter families: Archival resources and the history of the American eugenics movement, 1908-1930. Proceedings of the American Philosophical Society.

Smith, A. (1776). *The Wealth of Nations.*

# Mother of Exiles

by Caitlyn Zawideh
*From English 325: The Art of the Essay*
Nominated by Molly Beer

Caitlyn Zawideh's essay about the ICE incarceration of eighty members of Detroit's Chaldean community deftly integrates history, geography, current events, and her own Chaldean-American identity.

*Molly Beer*

# Mother of Exiles

*"We offer them three choices: Islam; the dhimma contract – involving payment of jizya; if they refuse this they will have nothing but the sword."*

On Friday, July 18, 2014, ISIS militants gave the Christian population of Mosul, Iraq, an ultimatum: pay a tax, convert to Islam, or die. By noon on July 19, for the first time in seventeen-hundred years, there was not a single Christian in the city (Rubin). ISIS gave this same ultimatum to Kurdish populations in other regions, in one case taking hostages and killing thousands on Mount Sinjar.

By August 7, ISIS captured most of Iraq's Nineveh province, displacing nearly all its residents, leaving them to sleep in churches, in cars, or on street sides. They destroyed Christian artifacts, removed crosses from churches and replaced them with their flag (Shlama Foundation).

Unequivocally, no group has suffered more at the hands of ISIS than Muslims. The specific and systematic nature of the violence against Christians, however, is what led Secretary of State John Kerry to declare these attacks an act of genocide less than a month after the capture of Mosul. Three years later, the Trump Administration continues to acknowledge the genocide of Iraqi Christians as ongoing (CSPAN). As a candidate, Trump gained the support of Iraqi Christians in the US in a speech condemning violence in the Middle East and promised that as president he will "reject bigotry and oppression in all its forms" (Politico).

The ISIS attack on Mosul was not the first time Iraqi Christians have been targeted and driven from their homes. In 1933, post-World War I, after the British left Iraq and in the wake of the fall of the Ottoman Empire, the Iraqi army slaughtered three thousand Iraqi Christians. In 1970, the Baathist government recognized the "legitimate rights of all minorities in the frame of Iraqi unity" in the constitution. This statement permitted the legal existence of five main Christian communities in Iraq. It allowed them to build churches and establish a clergy. Despite government censoring of their language in media publications, they maintained it in a limited capacity at home, church, and some classrooms. The right to exist was a step forward, but the theoretically secular Baathist government would not separate Islam from Arab culture. This left Christians marginalized, excluded from Arab culture, and powerless against the Iraq government. More recently, the Iraq War lead to a massive Exodus of Christians from the Middle East. The *New York Times* reported that from the fall of Saddam Hussein in 2003 to 2015 the Christian population of Iraq dropped from 1.5 million to less than 500 thousand (Griswold). According to CBS News, one and a half million Christians have been displaced to escape the threat of ISIS (CBS News).

*** 

My grandparents, Mosha and Nedju, left their village in Northern Iraq, home to a sect of Iraqi Christians called Chaldeans, in the 1960s. They had five kids and a considerable amount of land, but the government's persecution of non-Muslims gave them no choice but to leave. Mosha first came to America alone and worked on an assembly line for Chrysler until he saved enough to buy a small house in a mostly Chaldean neighborhood in Detroit. Then Nedju and their children joined him.

Mosha's brother, Salman, was one of the first to establish the Chaldean community in Michigan when he immigrated here in 1950. Salman, who had already practiced law for two years in Iraq, re-earned his Juris Doctorate so he could continue practicing in Michigan, becoming the first Chaldean lawyer in the state. In service of the Chaldean community, Salman laid down the legal ground work for many of the first Chaldean businesses. Today, sixty-one percent of Chaldeans are business owners (CACC). In service of the United States, he was an advisor to the American embassy in Iraq, worked with President Jimmy Carter's Administration on Iraqi diplomacy in 1979, and was on an advisory committee for George HW Bush during the Iraq Kuwait conflict in 1991 and leading up to the Gulf War. In 2009, he was awarded an Ellis Island Medal of Honor.

The opportunities America offers do not come without sacrifice. Salman, my grandparents, and thousands more Chaldeans like them had to leave behind a cultural history older than America itself. They left behind a history that stretches back so far back, 5500 years, that we have a biblical presence, linking us to the prophet Abraham in the book of Genesis: *Terah took Abram his son, and Lot the son of Haran, his grandson, and Sarai his daughter-in-law, his son Abram's wife; and they went out together from Ur of the Chaldeans in order to enter the land of Canaan; and they went as far as Haran, and settled there.* [11.31]

Chaldeans are descendants of ancient Assyrian and Babylonian civilizations whose existence began thousands of years before Jesus. In Mesopotamia, which covered regions of modern-day of Syria and Iraq, the Chaldeans were an indigenous tribe residing in what is today Northern Iraq. Ninety-five percent of Chaldeans can trace their lineage back to one village, Telkaif, where my grandparents were born.

Today, in Michigan and Iraq, religion is a central component of Chaldean culture. The story goes that in the first century, St. Thomas, one of Jesus' Twelve Apostles brought Christianity to Mesopotamia. Fracturing over disagreements on the authority of the pope and the nature of Jesus, Christianity split into different sects across the Middle East. The Chaldean Catholic Church was founded towards the end of the second century but was not united with the Roman Catholic Church until 1830. To be Chaldean is now inseparable from the Roman Catholic faith. Even our language, Sureth (older than ninety-five percent of languages currently spoken in the world), is a dialect of the ancient Aramaic language spoken by Jesus.

Mainly concentrated in metro Detroit, 121 thousand Chaldeans currently live in Michigan, with 150 thousand more living throughout the US (CACC). As a close-knit community, older Chaldeans are especially good at recognizing their own.

"What's your last name?" they ask. "You're from Telkaif, I can tell."

So you tell them your last name and your mom's last name and her dad's name, and you keep going until they recognize it, until they make a connection like "my second cousin, her brother-in-law, he was your Baba's neighbor back home."

I thought this was something unique to Chaldeans, but a friend once witnessed a waiter and me play this guess-the-relative game and called it "Dutch bingo." Apparently, the Dutch population in western Michigan, a community established by immigrants in the nineteenth century, is similarly connected.

The story of immigrants, like the story of my family, is at the heart of the American Dream. Inspired by her Uncle Salman, my mom chose to become a lawyer. Now, I am a sophomore at the University of Michigan, studying Computer Science. This wouldn't be an option if my grandparents had stayed in Iraq. They accomplished what all people hope to do: they gave their children their best shot at a good life. The idea that anyone can come to America and have this opportunity is a narrative that this country has always prided itself on but so often fails to live up to.

***

As a first grader staring at a scan-tron sheet for a standardized test, I raised my hand.

"What is it sweetie?" my teacher asked.

I pointed to the box labeled "Race."

"What am I?" I ask her. She paused in a moment, unsure, before telling me to select the box labeled "Other."

To this day there is some debate on what category Chaldeans fall under. On the census and on college applications, we are counted as White. My dad, who is not Chaldean, once said that we're Arab, that Iraq is geographically part of The Arab World, so we must be. My mom says Chaldeans have never been identified as Arab. My cousin, Chris, tells me none of it matters.

"If you go back far enough, we're all Assyrians." I tend to agree with him. However, I have always felt removed from the Chaldean community in Iraq.

Often when my family talks about Iraq, they say, "back home."

Iraq was never my home. Only my mom's side of the family is Chaldean. My dad is Jordanian, but growing up, my mom's side was the dominant cultural force. Although I am, technically, a second-generation immigrant, I often feel farther removed from my Chaldean heritage than that. Both my parents grew up in the United States. My mom was an infant when she left Iraq and remembers nothing of it. To me, being Chaldean has always had more to do with our community in the United States.

***

On Sunday, June 11, 2017, ICE agents detained around eighty men in the metro Detroit area, almost all of them Chaldean immigrants. They were taken to a federal building in Detroit, loaded onto a bus, and driven away – all while their families watched from the other side of a fence, screaming, protesting, demanding answers. Later, their families were informed that the detained individuals were taken to the Northeast Ohio Correctional Center to await deportation to Iraq. Similar raids took place across the United States, ICE specifically targeting Iraqi nationals (Chiaramonte).

The raids were a result of a deal between Iraq and the Trump Administration. Previously, Iraq refused to accept Iraqi nationals with orders of removal from the United States. In an effort to be excluded from President Trump's travel ban, the Iraqi government agreed to accept the decades old backlog of Iraqi immigrants in the US subject to deportation (Jarrett). For the Iraqi Christians in the US, specifically the Chaldean community in Michigan, the ICE raids came as a surprise, a violation of Trump's promise to protect Christians in the Middle East.

More than a betrayal, the raids are a human rights violation. If the individuals detained are deported to Iraq, where millions have already been displaced by the turmoil and violence in the country, where ISIS is specifically targeting and killing Christians, they will be thrown into immediate, life-threatening danger. More poignant still, the raids are a manifestation of America's failing immigrant narrative. The same country that once offered its immigrants freedom and safety is now delivering these men into the hands of their persecutors.

The families of the detained have been fighting to save their loved ones from deportations in the form or protests, petitions, and legal action. Immigration and the ethics of deportation is a messy and difficult topic. Here is the truth: The men arrested were in the United States legally but had at some point in their lives been convicted of a felony. They all served their sentences and the majority have kept a clean record since (Namou).

The men arrested committed their felonies as teens or in their twenties. Most of these crimes were non-violent, minor charges like marijuana possession, which would be a misdemeanor today, not a felony. Today they are in their 40s 50s and 60s. They are the parents, breadwinners, employers, and employees. They are old men who haven't seen Iraq in forty years, who have forgotten the language, who were so young when they left they don't have a single memory of "back home."

Deporting individuals who have violated the terms of their stay in the United States is not inherently unethical. However, to deport these men to is to put their lives in danger. In July, *Vox* and Detroit local news sources reported that a federal judge from Detroit, Mark A. Goldsmith, temporarily blocked the deportations due to extraordinary circumstance. In Goldsmith's words, "Each petitioner faces the risk of torture or death on the basis of residence in America and publicized criminal records. Many will also face persecution as a result of a particular religious affiliation" (Maizland).

This isn't about keeping criminals in the United States, this isn't even about entering the United States illegally. It is entirely unethical to deport an individual to a country where he will likely face violent and even deadly persecution. Uprooting members of a community that have been here for more than a generation is in not in line with Trump's promise to "reject bigotry and oppression" and is a stark contradiction to American ideals.

America, nation of immigrants, Mother of Exiles. This is the story I was taught from a young age. In first grade, sitting in a desk chair too high for my feet to touch the ground, I swung my light-up sneakers back and forth as my teacher attempted to explain America's complex history of immigration and assimilation to a classroom of five-year-old's. Inevitably, she turned to *School House Rock* to deliver the immigrant narrative in a neat, rosy package:

> It doesn't matter what your skin.
> It doesn't matter where you're from,
> Or your religion, you jump right in

That's the myth my grandparents wanted to be a part of when they left everything behind in Iraq to start a new life in America. Since they've left, the violence against Christians in the Middle East has only intensified. Thousands have been killed, entire villages leveled, millions displaced, families broken. The Chaldean community in America hurts for those who are still in Iraq, for the ones who do not want to leave the homeland Chaldeans have occupied for thousands of years. Now we're also terrified that those who left Iraq to escape persecution are at risk of being sent back.

Of course, the immigrant narrative is flawed in ways a first grader cannot understand. Most glaringly, viewing America as a country of immigrants excludes the heritages of both African Americans, brought here in chains, and Native Americans, a minority nearly wiped from existence in the name of building "the New World."

Flaws aside, America is now failing to live up to the narrative at all out of fear of "Other." In reality, these "others" are no different than any immigrant group in American history who left their home countries for safety, for opportunity, or for a better life for their family for generations to come. The Chaldean American community in Michigan formed with the same dream at its core, and we've been fortunate enough to accomplish it. Now, with eighty men behind bars awaiting deportation, that dream has been threatened.

As a candidate, President Donald Trump made a promise to protect

Christians in the Middle East, and many members of the Chaldean community believed him. Since June, the detainees have remained in a detention facility awaiting their court hearings. After six months in federal custody, the court only recently ruled to give them a chance at bond. The situation is still ongoing and many young Chaldean lawyers are working pro-bono to prevent the deportations. However, there is only so much they can do. The Trump Administration is endangering the people they vowed to protect out of fear, and until that changes, the Chaldean community can only wait. Wait for a court date. Wait for a miracle. Wait for the United States to live up to the values that our ancestors who arrived over a century ago and those who have just arrived in the last few decades came here for in the first place.

# Works Cited

CACC. "Community Overview." *Chaldean American Chamber of Commerce (CACC)*.

Chiaramonte, Perry "ICE arrests of Iraqi Christians in US cause detainee families to feel betrayed." *Fox News*, FOX News Network.

CSPAN. "President Trump complete remarks at National Prayer Breakfast (C-SPAN)." *YouTube*, YouTube, 2 Feb. 2017.

Griswold, Eliza. "Is This the End of Christianity in the Middle East?" *The New York Times*, The New York Times, 22 July 2015.

Jarrett, Laura, and Sophie Tatum. "Trump administration announces new travel restrictions." *CNN*, Cable News Network, 25 Sept. 2017.

Lori Lieberman. "Great American Melting Pot." *School House Rock*.

Maizland, Sarah Wildman and Lindsay. "A federal judge just halted the deportation of 1,400 Iraqis." *Vox*, Vox, 14 June 2017.

Namou, Weam. "Detained to be Deported." *Chaldean News*, 26 July 2017.

Rubin, Alissa J. "ISIS Forces Last Iraqi Christians to Flee Mosul." *The New York Times*, The New York Times, 18 July 2014.

Shlama Foundation. "Situation Timeline." *Shlama Foundation*, www.shlama. org/situation-timeline.html.

Staff, Politico, et al. "Full text: Donald Trump's speech on fighting terrorism." *POLITICO*, 15 Aug. 2016.

www.ingramcontent.com/pod-product-compliance
Lightning Source LLC
Chambersburg PA
CBHW070828250626
47170CB00006B/2253